Machiavelli and the Four Seasons

33 1/3 Global

33 1/3 Global, a series related to but independent from **33 1/3**, takes the format of the original series of short, music-based books and brings the focus to music throughout the world. With initial volumes focusing on Japanese and Brazilian music, the series will also include volumes on the popular music of Australia/Oceania, Europe, Africa, the Middle East, and more.

33 1/3 Japan

Series Editor: Noriko Manabe

Spanning a range of artists and genres—from the 1970s rock of Happy End to technopop band Yellow Magic Orchestra, the Shibuya-kei of Cornelius, classic anime series *Cowboy Bebop*, J-Pop/EDM hybrid Perfume, and vocaloid star Hatsune Miku—**33 1/3 Japan** is a series devoted to in-depth examination of Japanese popular music of the twentieth and twenty-first centuries.

Published Titles:

Supercell's *Supercell* by Keisuke Yamada

AKB48 by Patrick W. Galbraith and Jason G. Karlin

Yoko Kanno's *Cowboy Bebop Soundtrack* by Rose Bridges

Perfume's *Game* by Patrick St. Michel

Cornelius's *Fantasma* by Martin Roberts

Joe Hisaishi's *My Neighbor Totoro: Soundtrack* by Kunio Hara

Shonen Knife's *Happy Hour* by Brooke McCorkle

Nenes' *Koza Dabasa* by Henry Johnson

Yuming's *The 14th Moon* by Lasse Lehtonen

Toshiko Akiyoshi-Lew Tabackin Big Band's *Kogun* by E. Taylor Atkins

S.O.B.'s *Don't Be Swindle* by Mahon Murphy and Ran Zwigenberg

Forthcoming Titles:

Yellow Magic Orchestra's *Yellow Magic Orchestra* by Toshiyuki Ohwada

Kohaku utagassen: The Red and White Song Contest by Shelley Brunt

33 1/3 Brazil

Series Editor: Jason Stanyek

Covering the genres of samba, tropicália, rock, hip hop, forró, bossa nova, heavy metal and funk, among others, **33 1/3 Brazil** is a series devoted to in-depth examination of the most important Brazilian albums of the twentieth and twenty-first centuries.

Published Titles:

Caetano Veloso's *A Foreign Sound* by Barbara Browning
Tim Maia's *Tim Maia Racional Vols. 1 & 2* by Allen Thayer
João Gilberto and Stan Getz's *Getz/Gilberto* by Brian McCann
Gilberto Gil's *Refazenda* by Marc A. Hertzman
Dona Ivone Lara's *Sorriso Negro* by Mila Burns
Milton Nascimento and Lô Borges's *The Corner Club* by Jonathon Grasse
Racionais MCs' *Sobrevivendo no Inferno* by Derek Pardue
Naná Vasconcelos's *Saudades* by Daniel B. Sharp
Chico Buarque's First *Chico Buarque* by Charles A. Perrone

Forthcoming Titles:

Jorge Ben Jor's *África Brasil* by Frederick J. Moehn

33 1/3 Europe

Series Editor: Fabian Holt

Spanning a range of artists and genres, **33 1/3 Europe** offers engaging accounts of popular and culturally significant albums of Continental Europe and the North Atlantic from the twentieth and twenty-first centuries.

Published Titles:

Darkthrone's *A Blaze in the Northern Sky* by Ross Hagen
Ivo Papazov's *Balkanology* by Carol Silverman
Heiner Müller and Heiner Goebbels's *Wolokolamsker Chaussee* by Philip V. Bohlman

Modeselektor's *Happy Birthday!* by Sean Nye
Mercyful Fate's *Don't Break the Oath* by Henrik Marstal
Bea Playa's *I'll Be Your Plaything* by Anna Szemere and András Rónai
Various Artists' *DJs do Guetto* by Richard Elliott
Czesław Niemen's *Niemen Enigmatic* by Ewa Mazierska and Mariusz Gradowski
Massada's *Astaganaga* by Lutgard Mutsaers
Los Rodriguez's *Sin Documentos* by Fernán del Val and Héctor Fouce
Édith Piaf's *Récital 1961* by David Looseley
Nuovo Canzoniere Italiano's *Bella Ciao* by Jacopo Tomatis
Iannis Xenakis's *Persepolis* by Aram Yardumian
Vopli Vidopliassova's *Tantsi* by Maria Sonevytsky
Amália Rodrigues's *Amália at the Olympia* by Lila Ellen Gray
Ardit Gjebrea's *Projekt Jon* by Nicholas Tochka
Aqua's *Aquarium* by C.C. McKee
J.M.K.E.'s *To the Cold Land* by Brigitta Davidjants
Taco Hemingway's *Jarmark* by Kamila Rymajdo

Forthcoming Titles:

Tripes' *Kefali Gemato Hrisafi* by Dafni Tragaki
Silly's *Februar* by Michael Rauhut
CCCP's *Fedeli Alla Linea's 1964–1985 Affinità-Divergenze Fra Il Compagno Togliatti E Noi Del Conseguimento Della Maggiore Età* by Giacomo Bottà

33 1/3 Oceania

Series Editors: Jon Stratton (senior editor) and Jon Dale (specializing in books on albums from Aotearoa/New Zealand)

Spanning a range of artists and genres from Australian Indigenous artists to Maori and Pasifika artists, from Aotearoa/New Zealand noise music to Australian rock, and including music from Papua and other Pacific islands, 33 1/3 Oceania offers exciting accounts of albums that illustrate the wide range of music made in the Oceania region.

Published Titles:

John Farnham's *Whispering Jack* by Graeme Turner
The Church's *Starfish* by Chris Gibson
Regurgitator's *Unit* by Lachlan Goold and Lauren Istvandity
Kylie Minogue's *Kylie* by Adrian Renzo and Liz Giuffre
Alastair Riddell's *Space Waltz* by Ian Chapman
Hunters & Collectors's *Human Frailty* by Jon Stratton
The Front Lawn's *Songs from the Front Lawn* by Matthew Bannister
Bic Runga's *Drive* by Henry Johnson
The Dead C's *Clyma est mort* by Darren Jorgensen
Ed Kuepper's *Honey Steel's Gold* by John Encarnacao
Chain's *Toward the Blues* by Peter Beilharz
Hilltop Hoods' *The Calling* by Dianne Rodger
Screamfeeder's *Kitten Licks* by Ben Green and Ian Rogers
The Clean's *Boodle Boodle Boodle* by Geoff Stahl
The Avalanches' *Since I Left You* by Charles Fairchild
TISM's *Machiavelli and the Four Seasons* by Tyler Jenke
Soundtrack from *Saturday Night Fever* by Clinton Walker
John Sangster's *Lord of the Rings* Suite by Bruce Johnson

Forthcoming Titles:

5MMM's *Compilation Album of Adelaide Bands 1980* by Collette Snowden
The Triffids' *Born Sandy Devotional* by Christina Ballico
Crowded House's *Together Alone* by Barnaby Smith
INXS' *Kick* by Lauren Moxey
Sunnyboys' *Sunnyboys* by Stephen Bruel
Eyeliner's *BUY NOW* by Michael Brown
silverchair's *Frogstomp* by Jay Daniel Thompson
The La De Das' *The Happy Prince* by John Tebbutt
Gary Shearston's *Dingo* by Peter Mills
Kate Ceberano's *Brave* by Panizza Allmark
Robert Forster's *Danger in the Past* by Patrick Chapman

Various Artists' *A Truckload of Sky: The Lost Songs of David McComb* by Glenn D'Cruz
Dinah Lee's *Introducing Dinah Lee* by Kimberly Cannady
The Waifs' *Up All Night* by Rebecca Bennison

33 1/3 South Asia

Series Editor: Natalie Sarrazin

From the films of Bollywood and Lollywood, to home-grown *bhangra* hip-hop, Hindu devotional pop and Sufi rock, Sri Lankan rap, Indo jazz and disco, new-wave electronica and diasporic Asian Underground scene, **33 1/3 South Asia** takes readers on a sonically diverse journey through the most significant soundtracks and albums from the twentieth and twenty-first centuries.

Published:

Dil Chahta Hai Soundtrack by Jayson Beaster-Jones
Lata Mangeshkar's *My Favourites, Volume 2* by Anirudha Bhattacharjee and Chandrashekhar Rao
Coke Studio (Season 14) by Rakae Rehman Jamil and Khadija Muzaffar

Machiavelli and the Four Seasons

Tyler Jenke

Series Editor: Jon Stratton, UniSA Creative, University of South Australia, and Jon Dale, University of Melbourne, Australia

BLOOMSBURY ACADEMIC
NEW YORK • LONDON • OXFORD • NEW DELHI • SYDNEY

BLOOMSBURY ACADEMIC
Bloomsbury Publishing Inc
1385 Broadway, New York, NY 10018, USA
50 Bedford Square, London, WC1B 3DP, UK
29 Earlsfort Terrace, Dublin 2, Ireland

BLOOMSBURY, BLOOMSBURY ACADEMIC and the Diana logo are trademarks
of Bloomsbury Publishing Plc

First published in the United States of America 2025

Copyright © Tyler Jenke, 2025

For legal purposes the Acknowledgements on p.139 constitute an extension of
this copyright page.

All rights reserved. No part of this publication may be reproduced or transmitted
in any form or by any means, electronic or mechanical, including photocopying,
recording, or any information storage or retrieval system, without prior permission in
writing from the publishers.

Bloomsbury Publishing Inc does not have any control over, or responsibility for, any
third-party websites referred to or in this book. All internet addresses given in this
book were correct at the time of going to press. The author and publisher regret any
inconvenience caused if addresses have changed or sites have ceased to exist, but
can accept no responsibility for any such changes.

Whilst every effort has been made to locate copyright holders the publishers would
be grateful to hear from any person(s) not here acknowledged.

Library of Congress Cataloging-in-Publication Data

Names: Jenke, Tyler, author.
Title: Machiavelli and the four seasons / Tyler Jenke.
Other titles: TISM's Machiavelli and the four seasons
Description: [1.] | New York: Bloomsbury Academic, 2025. | Series: 33 1/3
Oceania | Includes bibliographical references.
Identifiers: LCCN 2024036283 (print) | LCCN 2024036284 (ebook) |
ISBN 9798765114094 (paperback) | ISBN 9798765114087 (hardback) |
ISBN 9798765114100 (ebook) | ISBN 9798765114117 (pdf)
Subjects: LCSH: TISM (Musical group). Machiavelli and the Four Seasons. |
Alternative rock music–Australia–History and criticism. |
Rock music–Australia–1991-2000–History and criticism.
Classification: LCC ML3534.6.A8 J46 2025 (print) | LCC ML3534.6.A8 (ebook) |
DDC 782.42166092/2–dcundefined
LC record available at https://lccn.loc.gov/2024036283
LC ebook record available at https://lccn.loc.gov/2024036284

ISBN: HB: 979-8-7651-1408-7
PB: 979-8-7651-1409-4
ePDF: 979-8-7651-1411-7
eBook: 979-8-7651-1410-0

Series: 33 1/3 Oceania

Typeset by Deanta Global Publishing Services, Chennai, India

To find out more about our authors and books visit www.bloomsbury.com
and sign up for our newsletters.

Contents

Introduction 1

1 **Form and meaning reach ultimate communion** 11

2 **The mystery of the artist explained** 35

3 *Machiavelli and the Four Seasons* 45

4 **The last Australian guitar hero** 105

5 **The art-income dialectic** 113

6 **40 years – Then death** 129

   Conclusion 133

Acknowledgements 139
Bibliography 141
Index 151

Introduction

Where, then, do TISM fit in? – 'Mourningtown Ride' (1992)

I've long been someone who claims the truth shouldn't stand in the way of a good story, though as a journalist, I acknowledge this flies in the face of that whole 'integrity' concept. For two decades, however, I've asserted I discovered Melbourne alternative collective TISM on the day they played their last show, in November 2004. The actual date was likely seven months later when they were the subject of a question on the Australian Broadcasting Corporation (ABC) quiz show *The Einstein Factor*. However, that story sounds nowhere near as impactful as if I told fellow fans I'd come onboard just as the ship began to sink.

However, that story isn't exactly truthful, either. While mention of the band on television did inspire my music-loving mother to tell me all she knew of this masked outfit, it was roughly a decade earlier I'd unknowingly had my first experiences with TISM.

Regardless of whenever the band made their presence felt within my life, I would have been wholly unaware this impending fondness for them would one day inspire my foray into the world of music journalism. It was their blending of music, humour, culture and verbosity that resonated deeply, and it was the desire to untangle the mysteries that surrounded the world of recorded sound that led to me putting pen to paper.

As the years went on, my journalism career would flourish, with TISM's command of songwriting and satire inspiring me along the way. Fittingly, opportunities to interview members of the band – both masked and unmasked – arrived, and in 2021, while serving as the editor of *Rolling Stone Australia*, I was suggested by a member to pen the liner notes to their *Collected Versus* compilation.

Despite my closeness to both their music and the written word, it wasn't until many years later I realized the parallels between the tales of my first experiences with TISM and the band themselves. Both are shrouded in mystery, both have public and private-facing versions, and both are malleable depending on the purpose they serve.

* * *

For decades, it was near-impossible to accurately tell the story of TISM. This was entirely by design, however. Much of the band's retelling of their history was purposely misleading, allowing half-truths and in-jokes to enter the narrative and germinating into rumours and innuendo, which still persist. As one journalist wrote in 1988 after being forced to interview the band in a flotation tank, 'TISM are not a band you find answers to. They are best left as an enigma.'[1]

Journalists attempting to uncover the truth about the band were made to adhere to ridiculous requests, often returning

---
[1] David Bruce, 'Behind a Band's Mask', *The Age EG*, 23 September 1988, 5.

with little more than a maddening story about their own experiences. One of their earliest interviews saw a writer taken to Richmond's Burnley Oval, where TISM stood 50 metres away holding a string. Responses were relayed via megaphone, but only if the string was held taut.[2]

Another was taken blindfolded to a commercial freezer, where he spoke to the group while running in an attempt to stave off hypothermia,[3] while others were forced to dress in a wetsuit in a St Kilda restaurant,[4] or were given answers taken verbatim from John Lennon's *Playboy* interview.[5]

While variables like their media appearances have fluctuated over the years, many constants have remained. Most notably are the costumes and masks the group have worn. Though the band's trademark look consists of largely black attire and a balaclava covering members' faces, a non-exhaustive list includes Ku Klux Klan uniforms made of newspaper, large suits to make them look like obese businessmen and various costumes featuring unwieldy headpieces.

Another constant is their intense live performances, of which the concepts are almost too numerous to name. Previous live shows have included onstage debates, operas, telethons and countless others. A performance for Channel 9's weekly variety television programme *Hey Hey It's Saturday* in 1989 saw the group's membership balloon to twenty-eight; an appearance

---

[2] Mara Smarelli, 'Taken for a Ride by Serious Mothers', *The Age EG*, 11 July 1986, 2.
[3] Craig Mathieson, 'TISM Break the Ice', *Beat* 216, 17 October 1990.
[4] Howard Stringer, 'Deep and Meaningless', *Rolling Stone Australia* 424, November 1988.
[5] TISM, *The TISM Guide to Little Aesthetics* (Melbourne: Stock, Aristotle & Waterman, 1989), 61.

at the opening of Melbourne's Virgin Megastore saw TISM distribute flyers for independent rival Gaslight Records; and a benefit for Melbourne community radio station 3RRR saw the band play for costs, resulting in them losing money.

The final show at Melbourne venue the Punters Club ended with TISM tearing fiberglass insulation out from the roof above the stage and showering it over the audience, while a performance at The Palace saw the group utilize the venue's two opposing stages, resulting in two iterations of the band performing alternately and simultaneously – to the dismay and confusion of the crowd.

The other notable constant in TISM's career is undoubtedly their identities and the mystique which surrounds them. The membership of the band has fluctuated and evolved both privately and publicly throughout its life but has revolved around seven core members – each occupying various roles and adopting pseudonyms which pluck from both ends of the cultural spectrum:

Humphrey B. Flaubert: Named for the French novelist Gustave Flaubert and children's television character Humphrey B. Bear, Flaubert is responsible for co-lead vocals, drum programming and sampling.

Ron Hitler-Barassi: Taking his moniker from the German dictator Adolf Hitler and the Australian rules footballer Ron Barassi, Hitler-Barassi shares lead vocals with Flaubert. Alongside reciting diatribes[6] during performances,

---

[6] A diatribe is defined as a lengthy, bitter speech which often uses humour and sarcasm in pursuit of criticizing its intended subject. Most spoken-word recitations from Hitler-Barassi are referred to as such, with the majority of live

Hitler-Barassi's intense live persona is also accompanied by occasional choreographed dancing.

Jock Cheese: The group's bassist and occasional guitarist, Cheese also adds his chameleonic vocals to a number of songs.

Eugene de la Hot-Croix Bun: Named for the French painter Eugène Delacroix, de la Hot-Croix Bun occupies the role of the group's keyboardist and occasional vocalist, with a handful of early press appearances also utilizing his accordion playing.

Jon St. Peenis: Named after the Australian entertainer John St Peeters, St. Peenis largely occupies the role of one of the band's dancers, though provides infrequent vocals and saxophone.

Les Miserables: Taking his name from Victor Hugo's 1862 novel *Les Misérables*, Miserables is one of the band's dancers. Two individuals have occupied the monikers of both St. Peenis and Miserables throughout the band's existence, with a personnel change occurring in the early 1990s.[7]

Tokin' Blackman: Initially known as **Tony Coitus**, after the American actor Tony Curtis, Blackman joined the group as their guitarist in 1991. Initially being given his pseudonym upon joining, Blackman chose his own name in mid-1995.

Leak Van Vlalen: Named for the American evolutionary biologist Leigh Van Valen, who proposed the Law of Extinction, Van Vlalen was the group's founding guitarist and also provided occasional vocals until his departure from the band in 1991.

---

shows featuring at least one which is often referenced to on the accompanying setlist as 'diatribe' regardless of any official title.
[7] Brett Buttfield, 'Crusaders for Citizen Average', *dB Magazine*, 1 March 1995.

Genre B. Goode: Named after Chuck Berry's 1958 single 'Johnny B. Goode', Goode was one of the band's founding members and mainly provided occasional vocals until his departure in around 1985.

These pseudonyms would be, for all intents and purposes, the 'true' identities of those under the masks, with the band officially making no mention of their 'real' identities publicly. As their profile grew and the need for anonymity increased, TISM would become the first and only band to have their names removed from the Australasian Performing Right Association (APRA) database, making them the only artist to be granted this level of privacy and anonymity by the organization.

Flaubert would again mask his identity as DC Root in his post-TISM band Root!, before acknowledging his past with The DC3's debut single 'I Was the Guy in TISM', and subsequently using his birth name for future projects. Blackman's name would be used upon his death in 2008,[8] and Cheese would perform in The Collaborators alongside Van Vlalen in 2018 under their birth names. The identities of de la Hot-Croix Bun, Goode, Hitler-Barassi, Miserables and St. Peenis have never been officially revealed.

Notwithstanding the fact that a public acknowledgement of any identities within the band may not have been forthcoming had the prospect of the band embarking on a reunion in 2022 seemed tangible, it is difficult to interview TISM in any capacity.

---

[8] Ron Hitler-Barassi, 'James Paull – Tism 1957-2008', *Smartartists Management*. http://www.smartartists.com.au/artists/jock.php, archived 2 May 2008, at the Wayback Machine.

Though Flaubert and Cheese are the only current members to discuss the band publicly under their real identities, their responses have traditionally been very considered, with little done to destroy the mystique that TISM curated. The group's long-held stance is to not discuss TISM in any official capacity when not 'in character', and therefore, any attempt to get official responses from the band outside of regular press engagements is a fool's errand.

Indeed, for the purposes of researching this volume, I unsuccessfully requested interviews with members of TISM. However, prior relationships with some of those behind the masks resulted in many off-the-record discussions, existing mainly to confirm the stories, facts and quotes offered up over the years. As such, almost all references to band members within this volume will be as the group initially intended, with stage names used instead of the real names they endeavoured to keep separate during the band's tenure.

However, conversations with those associated with the band – including producers Paul McKercher and Laurence Maddy, musician David Thrussell, former Shock Records CEO David Williams, comic artist Mark Sexton and comedian Tony Martin – were conducted and have greatly helped to inform this volume.

* * *

What follows is not a biography of TISM but rather an attempt to understand the story of the band and the album that made them into unlikely cult heroes within the Australian music scene.

Even with an attitude to their craft which could be equally described as singular and self-sabotaging, TISM managed to achieve what their critics might have deemed impossible in their earliest years. Indeed, after thirteen years together, the band managed to reach a level of mainstream success and acceptance with the release of *Machiavelli and the Four Seasons*.

Released in May 1995, TISM's third album represents their commercial and critical peak and heralded something of a sonic shift for the group. Abandoning plans of a harder guitar-based record for fears of becoming associated with grunge, the group shifted their approach, swapping traditional rock-based instrumentation for a sound more reliant on synthesizers and samplers. The result was a record which stood between two worlds – one which displayed their pub-rock (a distinctly Australian style of music which had originated in Melbourne and was made popular by names such as Billy Thorpe & the Aztecs in the early 1970s[9]) roots, and another which exhibited a band unafraid to remain musically progressive and appealing to a more youthful demographic.

Yet even a record bound for commercial success wasn't safe from TISM's own self-destructive approach to their craft. Notably, the record would feature no reference to the band, instead adopting a photograph of 1960s doo-wop outfit The Hollywood Argyles for its cover, sporting liner notes which established the band as an American pop group from 1963

---

[9] Paul Oldham, "'Suck More Piss': How the Confluence of Key Melbourne-Based Audiences, Musicians, and Iconic Scene Spaces Informed the Oz Rock Identity', *Perfect Beat*, January 2014, 121.

and listing a series of fake tracks whose names featured slight variations on the phrase 'I Love You Baby'.

So much was this viewed as a potential commercial misstep that the band's own label would affix stickers to the front of each album, assuring fans that 'This is actually a TISM album'.

Despite another attempt at what could equally be described as 'subversive artistic statement' or 'career suicide', TISM's daring venture into new musical territory was validated by its wider success. Peaking at #8 on the ARIA (the Australian Recording Industry Association) Albums Chart in June, the album would go Gold with sales in excess of 35,000 copies, and ultimately win Best Independent Release at the 1995 ARIA Awards.

In January 1996, three singles from the record would be voted into triple j's then-burgeoning Hottest 100 countdown, with popular tracks '(He'll Never Be An) Ol' Man River' and 'Greg! The Stop Sign!!' reaching #9 and #10, respectively. In 2021, the record's legacy would again be cemented when *Rolling Stone Australia* listed *Machiavelli* at #74 in its list of the '200 Greatest Australian Albums of All Time', while the band's 1988 debut, *Great Truckin' Songs of the Renaissance*, would reach #102.[10]

Machiavelli found itself launched into a music scene devoid of any sort of personality, with the radio-friendly, inoffensive sounds of Céline Dion, Roachford and Take That sitting atop the charts. With beat-driven dance music and disingenuous pop ballads driving sales, TISM's latest release was one that was exciting, dangerous and controversial. The record's lead single arrived as a sharp takedown of celebrity worship, with

---
[10] Tyler Jenke, '200 Greatest Australian Albums of All Time', *Rolling Stone Australia* 007, December 2021.

its lead chorus of 'I'm on the drug that killed River Phoenix' referencing the still-fresh passing of its namesake just eighteen months earlier.

By the mid-1990s, TISM were a band who seemed destined to continue with their comparatively safe approach of crafting rock music and pairing it with the sense of satire and disruption which had become associated with them, never once bothering to seriously compete with the world of pop music and its cult of personality. Of course, there's a sense of irony in how a band such as TISM, whose very aesthetic removed a sense of individual personality, managed to upend the contemporary style of popular music with their own brand of it.

However, as Hitler-Barassi had once opined, 'the greatest satirical statement that we could have made on the Australian rock industry is to actually become moderately successful within it'.[11] Who could have known that TISM, a group whose very existence seemed to be based around how far the limit could be pushed and how to actively avoid the spotlight, would briefly become one of the most visible Australian groups of the 1990s? Certainly not the fans, certainly not the critics but *certainly* not TISM.

---

[11] Brett Buttfield, 'The Hitler Diaries', *dB Magazine* 120, 5 June 1996.

1 Form and meaning reach ultimate communion

Fools suffered gladly by popular taste, look up with horror on their pretty face: They hear that name, all pretence is through – Just mention TISM, and they will say, 'Who?' – 'TISM Are Back' (2004)

It's difficult to talk about TISM without first touching upon the background against which they coalesced. Though Flaubert and Van Vlalen had known each other since attending primary school, it wasn't until 1976 when the pair first formed a band, serving as half of the short-lived quartet Abroz.[1] More of a loose concept than an actual band, this project soon gave way to Kestrel Hawk, which formed the ashes of Abroz after its members expressed a desire to be 'a proper rock band'[2] much like Led Zeppelin.

---

[1] Damian Cowell, 'Episode 4: Old Sneakers', *Only the Shit You Love: The Podcast*, 18 August 2021. https://podcasts.apple.com/au/podcast/podcast-3-episode-4-old-sneakers/id1585650286?i=1000535170120.
[2] Damian Cowell, 'Episode 6: Fucking Annoying', *Only the Shit You Love: The Podcast*, 1 September 2021. https://podcasts.apple.com/au/podcast/podcast-5-episode-6-fucking-annoying/id1585650286?i=1000535170121.

Unlike Led Zeppelin, however, Kestrel Hawk didn't break new ground. With Van Vlalen on guitar and Flaubert on drums despite aspirations for guitar or vocals, the quartet debuted at the Springvale High School Fete Talent Contest in 1977.[3] This group was also short-lived, with its seventeen-year-old members practising at Van Vlalen's home in the south-eastern Melbourne suburb of Springvale, largely emulating artists like Deep Purple, Crosby Stills Nash & Young and Status Quo – whose song 'Paper Planes' was the first the band ever performed live.[4]

Within a month of forming, Kestrel Hawk performed at the Noble Park Youth Club in December 1977. Sharing a bill with the Disco Duck Mobile Disco, the set was described by Van Vlalen as a 'shocker'[5] and Flaubert as 'frighteningly bad'.[6] The set also featured a cover of AC/DC's 'T.N.T.', a recording of which was later mixed into TISM's 2004 song 'Cerebral Knievel', and their 1995 cover of AC/DC's 'For Those About to Rock'.

Kestrel Hawk didn't last long beyond this ill-fated show, with the group's demise coinciding with their completion of high school. It also corresponded with the advent of Melbourne's famous Little Band Scene, which roughly existed from 1978 to 1981.[7] Largely known for its post-punk and experimental

---

[3] Damian Cowell, 'Episode 7: The Plot Thins', *Only the Shit You Love: The Podcast*, 8 September 2021. https://podcasts.apple.com/au/podcast/podcast-6-episode-7-the-plot-thins/id1585650286?i=1000535170032.
[4] Ibid.
[5] Sean Anthony Kelly, 'Noble Park Youth Club Dec77?!', Facebook, 20 November 2020. https://www.facebook.com/groups/44545772326/posts/10157643969512327/?comment_id=10157649762007327.
[6] Cowell, *Only the Shit You Love*, 8 September 2021.
[7] Alex Underwood, 'Looking Back at Melbourne's "Little Band Scene"', *Pilerats*, October 2016. http://pilerats.com/music/bands/looking-back-at-melbournes-little-band-scene/.

qualities, the Scene was launched by the Primitive Calculators, who inspired a movement for a deeply communal musical environment in which numerous small and short-lived bands would come and go.

Primitive Calculators essentially founded the scene when its members formed The Leapfrogs to open for their own set. This soon saw other 'little bands' forming as a result of friends or fellow musicians, with the vast majority of these groups releasing little – if any – recorded music. The Scene's underlying goal was one in pursuit of artistic expression rather than financial gain. Though short-lived in its existence, it was immortalized in Richard Lowenstein's 1986 film *Dogs in Space*, and impacted the changing attitudes of Melbourne's musical landscape – particularly the post-punk scene.[8]

For Flaubert, the Little Band Scene was emblematic of the 'coolness' he wished to achieve and the 'hip' crowd he'd wished to infiltrate. Admitting he was 'so far removed from cool',[9] he wasn't even sure what sort of music he was *supposed* to enjoy, his musical journey was largely independent thanks to the scene surrounding him. Long-time school friend and keyboardist de la Hot-Croix Bun recommended groups such as Steely Dan, which inspired Flaubert to look past the era's ubiquitous guitar sounds and discover energetic new bands which would result in a 'punk rock conversion'.[10]

---

[8] Ibid.
[9] Damian Cowell, 'Episode 11: Whatever Happened to Jessie's Girl?', *Only the Shit You Love: The Podcast*, 6 October 2021. https://podcasts.apple.com/au/podcast/podcast-10-episode-11-whatever-happened-to-jessies-girl/id1585650286?i=1000537679311.
[10] Ibid.

By 1980, Flaubert, Van Vlalen and de la Hot-Croix Bun had formed a new band with Kestrel Hawk bassist and vocalist Greg Wilmot. Naming themselves Tall Stories, Flaubert admitted that they were 'playing really well' but lacked any notion of 'which kind of band we wanted to be'.[11]

'With four people pulling in different directions, you might get a Jackson Pollock canvas of colours', Flaubert recalled. 'Or in our case, a sort of nothingy-grey.'[12]

In early 1980, frequent visitations of Caulfield's London Tavern led to a meeting with Private Club, a group which featured guitarist Cheese, who also played in the Sewer Rats. With Wilmot departing the band, Cheese was recruited into Tall Stories as his replacement.

Cheese recalled:

> They got me in, and they needed a bass player, so I went from guitar to bass and I approached that instrument like my approach to guitar. I actually wasn't happy being a bass player – I played it more percussively and more melodically.[13]

This new addition didn't solidify their musical direction, and after a handful of shows supporting bands such as The Jetsonnes (from whose ashes would form Hunters & Collectors

---

[11] Damian Cowell, 'Episode 12: Don't Bring Me Down, Proust', *Only the Shit You Love: The Podcast*, 13 October 2021. https://podcasts.apple.com/au/podcast/damian-cowell-only-the-shit-you-love-the-podcast/id1585650286.

[12] Damian Cowell, 'Episode 13: Wot Lionel Ritchie Said', *Only the Shit You Love: The Podcast*, 20 October 2021. https://podcasts.apple.com/au/podcast-12-episode-13-wot-lionel-ritchie-said/id1585650286?i=1000539134288.

[13] Tyler Jenke, 'Former TISM Member Jack Holt Unmasks for New Band, the Collaborators', *Tone Deaf*, 3 December 2018. https://tonedeaf.thebrag.com/former-tism-member-unmasks-collaborators/.

in 1981)[14] and The Riptides (a Brisbane power pop band who received attention for their pioneering 1979 single 'Sunset Strip'), the group slowly petered out, largely due to a lack of outside interest.[15]

Cheese's addition to the band effectively heralded the beginning of their next era, which officially began in late 1982 when the quartet reformed as I Can Run. Inspired by Flaubert's burgeoning love of post-punk and new wave, the band weren't as serious as the 'experimental bands' with 'barely listenable music'[16] that dominated the Little Band Scene of the time. Future manager Gavan Purdy would later call TISM's early days a 'reaction against all that post-Birthday Party stuff', in reference to the ubiquitous Nick Cave-fronted Melbourne post-punk group.[17]

Flaubert recalled:

> Post-punk wore art on its sleeve and desperately wanted you to know it. Some of the most pretentious old crap imaginable. And into this heady soup of wankery came a new band, formed out of the ashes of the terminally-doomed Tall Stories, a band with a meaningless, pointless, but vaguely arty name; I Can Run.[18]

---

[14] Jon Stratton, *Human Frailty* (New York: Bloomsbury Academic, 2023), 5.
[15] Cowell, *Only the Shit You Love*, 20 October 2021.
[16] Damian Cowell, 'Episode 14: Greta the Garbo', *Only the Shit You Love: The Podcast*, 27 October 2021. https://podcasts.apple.com/au/podcast/podcast-13-episode-14-greta-the-garbo/id1585650286?i=1000539820141.
[17] Clinton Walker, *Stranded: The Secret History of Australian Independent Music 1977–1991* (Sydney: Pan Macmillan, 1996), 190.
[18] Cowell, *Only the Shit You Love*, 27 October 2021.

In typically murky fashion, I Can Run can be considered analogous to TISM's formation. The group's official history pinpoints their 'hatching' in late 1982,[19] with their first recording made in December of that year – the same month that I Can Run played their first of seven shows.

At some point over the coming months, de la Hot-Croix Bun briefly left to travel overseas. The group would continue in his absence, with I Can Run's sound transforming into one described by Van Vlalen as being more 'angular', and reminiscent of bands like Gang of Four.[20] Upon de la Hot-Croix Bun's return, the 'pop keyboard sensibilities'[21] which would earmark much of TISM's earliest songs were put on full display.

Following I Can Run's final show in July 1983, Flaubert continued creating, working with Serious Young Insects' Mark White to record his first solo album – which remains unreleased. Alongside session percussion work, Flaubert auditioned for bands such as The Horla, a short-lived group founded by future Crowded House bassist Nick Seymour, and Synthetic Dream, which resulted in his involvement for two shows – the second featuring Van Vlalen on guitar.[22]

Three years earlier, Flaubert had begun studying English at Monash University, undertaking the same degree as

---

[19] TISM, *The TISM Guide to Little Aesthetics*, 1.
[20] Kieran Butler, 'This Is Treachery Sadly - A Podcast with Leak Van Vlalen (TISM)', YouTube, 20 November 2022. https://www.youtube.com/watch?v=NDNMWtdncXg.
[21] Ibid.
[22] Damian Cowell, 'Episode 16: Hamster Grammar Rocks Your Party', *Only the Shit You Love: The Podcast*, 10 November 2021. https://podcasts.apple.com/au/podcast/podcast-15-episode-16-hamster-grammar-rocks-your-party/id1585650286?i=1000541293678.

Hitler-Barassi, who he had met through the latter's older brother. Describing their friendship as close and their sense of humour and worldview as 'very singular',[23] Flaubert admitted that his 'very serious ambition to be a proper serious rockstar'[24] while performing in a 'no-hoper garage band'[25] was greatly influenced by the non-musical Hitler-Barassi's decision to write his own lyrics. Said Flaubert:

> That moment, those lyrics on that piece of paper – that sort of bird-like scrawling that he did – that changed his life and changed my life because that sort of set in motion the juggernaut that became TISM.[26]

The moment at which Hitler-Barassi's lyrics were written can be viewed as 'the big bang' from which TISM exploded out into the world and the moment in which its members effectively became their alter egos.

Much of the nascent band's early days were spent at Hitler-Barassi's house in the south-eastern Melbourne suburb of Wheelers Hill, which served as a hangout where many formative ideas were shared. Flaubert and Hitler-Barassi made the decision to record a cassette of music, with its personnel comprising those present at the time. The initial cassette,

---

[23] Adam Zwar, 'TISM'S Damian Cowell', *Out of the Question with Adam Zwar*, 16 December 2015. https://omny.fm/shows/10-questions-with-adam-zwar/10-questions-with-adam-zwar-tisms-damian-cowell.
[24] Ibid.
[25] Ibid.
[26] Ibid.

dubbed *Great Truckin' Songs of the Renaissance*[27] and recorded in December 1982, also featured Cheese, Van Vlalen, de la Hot-Croix Bun and former Tall Stories member Wilmot. Wilmot's fleeting appearance was barely immortalized, with the extent of his presence amounting to little more than dismissive giggling and slight acoustic guitar.[28]

This tape was recorded in the rumpus room of their hangout, with the fluid and communal nature of the recording meaning that friends would come and go depending on availability. The band's final line-up solidified when the decision to book a gig under the TISM name was made, at which point those at the recording sessions who could not play an instrument or simply provided occasional vocals departed.

Per Van Vlalen's later recollection, TISM was viewed as the 'retirement band', and one that wouldn't result in as much focus as their earlier groups: 'We were going, "This is no good, this is too hard, let's go and have our professional careers and we'll have this silly band on the side."'[29]

While TISM can simultaneously be viewed as both analogous and an entirely separate entity to the more serious I Can Run, elements of the future can be found within the past thanks to the presence of progressively humorous stage banter at I Can Run's live shows. Unlike I Can Run, TISM's entire raison d'être was one of fun, whereas it had previously been tamped down so as to be taken seriously by the 'cooler' crowd.

---

[27] This cassette is entirely separate to their 1988 debut album of the same name.
[28] The credits to 'Yassa Arathin-A-Go-Go' on the 2002 compilation *Best Off* list an individual named L'Touzin as being responsible for 'Barely Audible Giggling'.
[29] Kieren Butler and Sean Kelly, 'RealiTISM', *Station 59*, Melbourne, 14 April 2012.

Initially choosing names such as The Men from Unco, The Go-Code and Botty Terror, the origins behind the final moniker, This Is Serious Mum, can vary depending on who is telling the story. While one origin story posits the name emerged from words uttered to members' parents while defending their choices to pursue music over more pertinent matters, another tale claims that it sparked from a discussion with close friend Terri Rowe at the Wheelers Hill house about the most 'uncool' thing in one's life. Ultimately, This Is Serious Mum was chosen due to the unfashionable nature associated with having a band name that included the word 'mum'.

The members, however, soon found themselves growing tired of the moniker's longer form, instead preferring the non-specific and vaguely ideological TISM. The name would officially stick when the band went on a co-headlining tour of Victoria, South Australia and New South Wales with Big Pig in 1986. With the long version of their name making them appear as the support band, it was shortened to TISM to fit on the poster and give the appearance of equal billing.[30]

* * *

Much of the inspiration that helped foster TISM in their early days undoubtedly comes from American art collective The Residents. Initially formed in 1969 as an unnamed entity, the band carved out a reputation for their unconventional song structures, singular aesthetic, largely anonymous existence and bizarre live performances.

---

[30] Butler and Kelly, 'RealiTISM', 7 April 2012.

Their *The Third Reich 'n Roll* album was released in 1976 and received attention for not only the Nazi imagery adorning its cover but the accompanying music video featuring the band performing in Ku Klux Klan outfits made of newspaper. These costumes influenced TISM's members when, around 1982, a handful of them would attend a themed party in which attendees dressed as their heroes. Choosing to dress as The Residents, they spent a day designing the costumes, which empowered their wearers with a newfound sense of anonymity and the power that it wielded.

Indeed, the work that resulted from TISM's earliest years was equally as avant-garde as The Residents themselves. Musically, much of their work took on a Dadaist approach,[31] bending the rules of what could be considered traditional art with an 'anti-art' perspective,[32] and often intending to equally offend and confound while taking part in the more traditional musical discipline. Likewise, live performances would adopt Brechtian techniques[33] by way of their limited interaction with the audience, and use of placards to convey song titles.

---

[31] Originating in Switzerland, Dadaism was a post First World War artistic movement which rejected the established rules of art and used a sense of anarchic defiance to critique and ridicule the very culture in which the art world existed. In keeping with the nonsensical and absurd nature of Dadaist art, many artists involved within the initial movement would also later be involved in the Surrealism movement.

[32] Hans Richter, *Dada: Art and Anti-Art* (London: Thames & Hudson, 1965), 7.

[33] Bertolt Brecht was a German playwright who is heavily associated with the concept of 'epic theatre', which challenges conventional theatre techniques and instead seeks to alienate the audience. Rather than allowing an audience to suspend their disbelief, Brecht attempted to take viewers out of their comfort zone by forcing them to partake in critical thinking in relation to his work.

Recalled Hitler-Barassi:

> The Residents were one of those groups that you were always glad they were around. I remember seeing them at The [Seaview] Ballroom when they came out [in 1986], and everything was considered. The live show was not just a live show, it had a sense of theatre and drama. The PR was manufactured. Even the albums, you could tell, had a very strong and unusual stance. I don't know if they directly influenced us, but we're very similar. I think that there is nothing that TISM does that isn't strongly manufactured.[34]

The similarities were also seen from an external point of view. In 1986, the *Sydney Morning Herald* described TISM as 'a cross between Skyhooks, Dave Warner, Talking Heads and The Residents,'[35] while a 1987 gig review likened them to 'Devo, The Residents and Stump'.[36]

However, there was an equally strong desire to construct songs which existed within the traditional pop music world, and to push the limits of the avant-garde by embracing the concept dubbed 'Z-Sharp'. This concept, named for a non-existent key signature and eagerly supported by members such as Cheese and Van Vlalen, would see them craft music in the same vein as Captain Beefheart and Frank Zappa.

'I made a rule in the old days of; "just don't play anything standard", Cheese later explained. 'Never play anything

---

[34] Ian Bennington, 'Return of the Pop Vigilantes', *Tabula Rasa*, February 2002, 18.
[35] Stuart Coupe, 'Rockers in Caverns Alive and Thriving', *The Sydney Morning Herald*, 20 July 1986, 117.
[36] David O'Neill, 'Live Review: This Is Serious Mum?, The Moffs, The Spliffs', *Juke* 635, 27 June 1987.

standard and always find a way to play it *differently* to the standard.'[37]

'Eckermann is Very Silly', the opening track to TISM's first cassette recording, exemplifies this approach, with detuned strings and atonal solos pairing with traditionally melodic songwriting from Flaubert and de la Hot-Croix Bun to craft something wholly unique.

Recalled former manager Michael Lynch:

> I think they came through a different strain, and people have quoted what those strains are, like The Residents and Devo. They just didn't want to be an art-rock band or an experimental band, they wanted to be a pop band, and be a bit more high energy about it – and a bit more confrontational.[38]

The roots of this can be traced back to Tall Stories and I Can Run's origins within the often discordant post-punk scene, which had finessed by the time that TISM formed. While Tall Stories would see the group getting together and jamming in the same room, TISM's approach began similarly but gradually grew to be more independent, with music and lyrics often being written separately and later joined at rehearsal.

While their earlier material would be considered stronger and more resonant by the band due to this communal creative process, that's not to discount the commercial success that resulted from a more disjointed and independent one.

---

[37] Tyler Jenke, 'Ex-TISM Member Jack Holt Talks the Debut of His New Band, the Collaborators', *Tone Deaf*, 23 October 2019. https://tonedeaf.thebrag.com/jack-holt-the-collaborators-album-live-interview.

[38] Michael Lynch, Interview with John Safran, *The J Files*, triple j, 27 August 2015.

However, one of the most prominent driving forces behind TISM's creative process was the enduring slogan, 'Wouldn't it be good if...?'[39] It was this sort of approach, to be spontaneous and to pursue ideas for their enjoyment rather than commercial potential, that allowed TISM to follow in the footsteps of The Residents.

This approach would also flow into TISM's lyrics. Lyrically, the band would seem almost paradoxical due to subject matter which ranged from the highly literate to the intensely juvenile. References to famed literary figures would sit alongside mentions of pop culture icons, football players and politicians, while adolescent humour would be just as present within their unique approach, which was more akin to surrealist pop. Though their songwriting would undoubtedly evolve throughout their career, the highly literate qualities, mixed with references to pop culture, sports and Melbourne-centric locations would become noted constants.

Hitler-Barassi sarcastically stated the main reason for their use of literary references was due to 'trying to make everyone else aware that we are probably far more intelligent than them'. Flaubert, however, jovially countered by noting 'the paltry literary references we put in our songs are merely there just to impress our fans even though we don't understand them ourselves'.[40]

Such an obsession with their use of Melbourne-centric locations, popular culture figures and literary references

---

[39] Damian Cowell, 'The Birth of Uncool: How TISM Gatecrashed Melbourne Music', *Vimeo*, 20 March 2014. https://vimeo.com/89629916.
[40] Clinton Porteous, 'This Is This Is Serious Mum', *Waves* 81, December 1986.

may also be in part due to the band's attempts to reckon with their suburban existence. In much the same way Perth's Dave Warner would document his fundamentally ambivalent relationship with suburbia,[41] TISM would themselves address their own preoccupation with the outer suburbs in their work.

Though calling Springvale their home, TISM's avant-garde sensibilities positioned themselves as a band best suited for the comparatively more literate surroundings of Melbourne (or perhaps the post-punk hub of St Kilda), though their suburban roots would often see them blend elements of lower-class masculine bravado with critiques of the inner-city intelligentsia who dared to take art too seriously.

Despite frequent performances away from major cities and naming their 1992 extended play (EP) *The Beasts of Suburban*, TISM's non-metropolitan position was often unsettled, given the fact that the suburban base of their songs – including its very subject matter – was often held up for attack and criticism. One prominent example is Hitler-Barassi's name, which equates AFL footballer Ron Barassi with German dictator Adolf Hitler.

While some members of TISM did in fact hold university degrees and appeared inclined to take on a far more artistic approach to art than their suburban upbringing may stereotypically allow, those roots have forever remained evident within their canon. 'Pub car parks, I think, are a big

---

[41] Dave Warner's relationship with suburbia is documented by way of songs such as 1976's 'Suburban Boy' and the name of his band, Dave Warner's From The Suburbs.

influence on our work', Hitler-Barassi noted in 2004. 'You cannot underestimate the cultural significance of a head hitting the asphalt of a car park at high velocity', added Flaubert. 'Being part of that sort of environment, I think, enriches your art.'[42]

Additionally, TISM would also disdain being labelled a 'joke band', with Hitler-Barassi noting their reasons for injecting satire and humour into their music were often misinterpreted:

> Our position to ourselves is a position of satire. It does get tiresome when you're not granted that as a legitimate position. It annoys me. I don't mind if you don't like TISM. I don't mind if you don't like the music. I do mind if the position that we take, which is one of satire, is seen as the equivalent of a joke band. Suddenly you're Weird Al' Yankovic [. . .] I think satire is a legitimate stance to take vis-a-vis your audience and your art as any other. If there's a fuckin' industry crying out for fuckin' satire, I tell you it's the rock 'n' roll industry. Someone's gotta lay the boot in, and we're the sort of cowardly pricks who'll do that for you.[43]

Regardless, it was the combination of the music, satire, lyrics, live performances, antagonistic behaviour, confronting appearance and general mastery of all facets that would come to define the very modus operandi of TISM. While some bands would rely on one aspect of their existence being the hook

---
[42] TISM, 'TISM Explained', *The White Albun* (Genre B. Goode/Madman, 2004).
[43] Adam Ford, 'Adam Ford Interviews Ron Hitler Barassi', *Frisbee*, 1998/*Duck Fat* 2, 1999. https://www.oocities.org/tismselfstorage/duckfat.html.

that draws in fans, TISM's 'firing on all cylinders' approach meant they were attacking from all creative fronts simultaneously.

* * *

By the end of 1983, a number of cassette tapes had been recorded under the TISM moniker, and I Can Run had reached its unheralded end. However, prior to the band's dissolution, a preview of what was to come had been provided at two of I Can Run's gigs, with Hitler-Barassi, Miserables and Goode appearing in costume during I Can Run's sets to perform a handful of songs from these early cassettes.

On 6 December 1983, the first TISM performance officially took place. Dubbed the 'Get Fucked Concert', attendees were lured to the show at the Duncan Mackinnon Reserve in the south-eastern Melbourne suburb of Murrumbeena by handtyped invitations describing the event as both the 'farewell gig' and 'genesis of a revolutionary new synthesis of art, music and self-abuse'.[44] The band would later claim they intended to refrain from live performances due to both their 'hitherto unbreakable vow of total obscurity'[45] and belief in 'the pristine virginity of obscurity', only to be convinced otherwise by Rowe.[46]

Recollections of this debut performance are scarce, and only scant footage has been made public – featuring two members of TISM dressed in newspaper Ku Klux Klan outfits during a rendition of 'The Art-Income Dialectic'.[47] Perhaps one

---

[44] TISM, 'Get Fucked Concert', invitation, 1983.
[45] TISM, '*T*I*S*M*', media release, July 1985.
[46] Porteous, 'This Is This Is Serious Mum'.
[47] TISM, 'The Art-Income Dialectic', *The White Albun* (Genre B. Goode/Madman, 2004).

of the reasons no more footage has been made available is that while three members were dressed in the costumes, four others were not.

While the somewhat captive audience of invitees listened intently to the shambolic concert, the naïveté of the band was on full display, with Flaubert's Roland TR-606 drum machine being louder than planned, the vocals being lost in the mix and the audience instead just seeing three men in confronting costumes performing rudimentary dance moves.

Officially, TISM split following the 'artistic and commercial failure'[48] that was this performance, though they continued to exist privately. More tapes were made, and between February and August 1984, a number of songs were recorded, largely with Serious Young Insects' Mark White. These tracks were collected onto a self-titled cassette, which has since been erroneously referred to as a demo tape.

On 25 November 1984, TISM played a twenty-minute set at Melbourne University's Tin Alley Bazaar, with their appearance organized by Flaubert's then-girlfriend.[49] If their invite-only Get Fucked Concert was to be viewed as their debut and farewell concert, this was the first in their series of 'reunion gigs' and ostensibly their first public performance.

This would later be viewed as the first real performance of TISM, with the Get Fucked Concert not being considered representative of their future selves. A box of the tapes was offered for sale at a market stall, with all having sold

---
[48] TISM, *The TISM Guide to Little Aesthetics*, 1.
[49] David Roy Williams, *This Is Serious Mum* (sleeve notes, Genre B. Goode/DRW, 2021).

by the end of the set, and giving the group a glimpse at commercial viability.

One of these tapes was passed to Paul Stewart, the frontman of contemporary Melbourne pub-rock group Painters and Dockers, who in turn handed it to Michael Lynch of VAMP booking agency, where local promoters Mark Burchett and Gavan Purdy worked.[50] Purdy was taken by TISM's lyricism, humour and 'electro-punk' musicality enough to take a chance on the band and helped get them onto the bottom of the bill at St Kilda's Prince of Wales on 1 August 1985, for their free Thursday night concerts. Purdy recalled:

> They were all super into it and they were into exploring what could happen with the band, but it wasn't like they were depending on the band to get up in the morning. They all had burgeoning careers in different professions, all university educated, but they were really good friends and they were doing what they thought was fun.[51]

Following the band's winning appearance at 3RRR's Battle of the Bands competition in November 1985, Purdy would take on the role of the band's manager, releasing their debut single, 'Defecate on My Face', in July 1986 via his own Elvis Records label.

With lyrics pertaining to Adolf Hitler's alleged coprophilia, the vinyl itself was equally inaccessible to the mainstream.

---

[50] Gavan Purdy and Augustus Billy, 'What It Was like to Manage Tism in the 1980s', *Beat Magazine*, 20 July 2021. https://beat.com.au/what-it-was-like-to-manage-tism-in-the-1980s-from-former-manager-gavan-purdy-himself/.
[51] Ibid.

Pressed onto 7" vinyl and packaged in a 12" sleeve with all sides glued shut, the single was paired with a fact sheet which outlined the band's history. Alongside the Dadaist writings, it finished with a cynical take on the band's approach to the music industry: 'This Is Serious Mum are very prepared to exchange their ideals for as much money as you would care to offer.'[52]

In November 1986, TISM released their debut EP, *Form and Meaning Reach Ultimate Communion*, which had begun life as a three-track single but was later expanded into a seven-track release. The EP's release was supported by a national tour alongside Big Pig, allowing TISM to take their sound outside of Melbourne for the first time. The resulting reviews of both the band's recorded output and live shows were enough for *The Sydney Morning Herald* to claim, 'there is no other band in the country (possibly the world) quite like TISM.'[53]

TISM's momentum continued with a win for Most Original New Band at the 3RRR/Najee Rock Awards in February 1987, and the recording of their next single, '40 Years – Then Death'. Despite the non-commercial approach of removing any indication of the band's name by being pressed on clear vinyl and packaged in a clear sleeve, the single was well-received, and by January 1988, they'd begun to record their debut album, the 'preposterously self-indulgent'[54] *Great Truckin' Songs of the Renaissance*.

---

[52] TISM, '*T*I*S*M*'.
[53] Gerry O'Shea, 'Vinyl Talk', *The Sydney Morning Herald*, 4 January 1987, 96.
[54] TISM, '*T.I.S.M. - Why??*', media release, May 1995.

Ambitious for a debut record, the double album comprised two halves. The first featured twelve songs – five of which were released as singles, alongside a re-recorded version of 'Defecate on My Face' – which captured the band's grasp on verbose pop rock. The other half of the album was subtitled 'This Record Is Not as Good as the Other One', and lived up to the promise for casual listeners. Alongside portions of bizarre radio appearances, live recordings and lengthy diatribes, the album finished with the eight-minute studio track 'Morrison Hostel' – a volatile critique of US rock band The Doors' late frontman Jim Morrison – and a recitation of album credits.

Released on 26 September 1988, via the Elvis Records label and distributed by Musicland Independent Distributors, the album received modest success. Despite a one-star review from *Rolling Stone*, it was named Molly Meldrum's album of the week on *Hey Hey It's Saturday*, entered the ARIA charts at its peak of #48 on 30 October and was bolstered by a win for Best Independent Release at the 1989 ARIA Awards for 'I'm Interested in Apathy'.

By the time of *Truckin' Songs*' release, TISM's presence within the Melbourne music scene was well known, with their enigmatic performances drawing attention for their intense and confronting nature. Worth noting, however, is the disproportionately male crowds the band drew.

Though TISM had emerged from an environment like the Little Band Scene, whose very existence was fluid and gender-diverse, the band's all-male line-up could have been seen as alienating to the group's female fanbase. However, casual observers would have seen that the band's lyrics and performances were indeed satirizing the notions of male bravado and toxic masculinity at the time.

While their shows were absent of any women in a performance aspect, TISM did, however, feature women as part of their stage show concepts or as rare vocalists. While Rebecca Barnard sang on a cover of 'The Judaeo-Christian Ethic' with then-partner and future Rebecca's Empire bandmate Shane O'Mara in 1991,[55] largely unheard songs like 'If You Want the Toilet, You're In It' and 'When Jesus Comes' also featured uncredited female vocals.[56]

Though the social and educational circles from which the band was formed are the main reason for an absence of female members, Flaubert succinctly addressed the question in 2001, claiming there are no women in TISM 'because they've seen our male fans'.[57]

* * *

By the late 1980s, the accompanying TISM live experience had also managed to solidify itself. In the early days, the band found it somewhat difficult to engage with fans, with Flaubert remembering their 1985 appearance at the Prince of Wales' 'scummy'[58] free Thursday night being earmarked by the need to convince otherwise uninterested punters:

---

[55] Shane O'Mara would also be responsible for introducing TISM to future guitarist Tokin' Blackman that same year.
[56] It's unclear why these vocals are uncredited, though given that TISM rarely referred to individual group members within their album credits, it may have been a conscious decision to not have the group referred to as anything but a single entity.
[57] Humphrey B. Flaubert, 'Q&A', *The Herald Sun*, 15 November 2001, 35.
[58] Rachel Hill, 'Shy, Enigmatic, or Just Plain Arrogant?', *The Canberra Times: Good Times*, 16 March 1995, 4.

We thought 'Christ, how are we going to stop these people from drinking?' so we marched through the room banging a small drum and ranting something mantra-like.[59]

As the band's image slowly became solidified with all-black outfits featuring balaclavas and yellow shooting glasses, this soon gave way to more costumes and onstage behaviour that was utilized in the pursuit of being both confronting and entertaining.

The decision for the band to hide their faces, largely through the use of balaclavas, partially came from a sense of self-preservation given they were all gainfully employed as blue- and white-collar workers, and also from the sense of unease and confrontation it provided the audience.[60]

Another benefit was the removal of any sense of identity that would take away from the TISM experience. One journalist suggested the masks were used 'so that people cannot associate them with anyone or anything. From this alienated position, they can present a critique of society which is not caught in the web of our own'.[61]

Despite this, the masks would ironically overshadow the band to some degree, becoming a point of frustration in interviews. 'There's never been a red herring more powerful than the fucking masks. It's drama, theatre', said Hitler-Barassi

---

[59] Ibid.
[60] The confronting and alienating response that came from the use of balaclavas was largely due to their association with burglars, though some comparisons were also made to their use by the Provisional Irish Republican Army.
[61] Clinton Porteous, 'This Is Serious Mum', *Rolling Clone/Lot's Wife*, 20 October 1988, 31.

in 1998. 'The masks are there to position ourselves unlike any other band. But we don't want you to see underneath the mask, we want you to see beyond the mask.'[62]

As Flaubert would later summarize, 'The anonymity of TISM is the one thing about us that is boring; it is there because there is nothing interesting underneath.'[63]

Slowly, the spectacle and the band's subversive image would become as much a part of the performance as the music itself, with shows featuring increasingly elaborate costumes and onstage antics such as art shows, fashion parades, faux stock exchanges and more. One concert, in the wake of New Zealand-born singer Ricky May's passing in June 1988, saw a dead pig (in reference to the late musician's weight) hung from the ceiling of The Club in Collingwood, dressed in a white shirt with a trumpet driven into its gut. Hitler-Barassi hugged the swaying pig carcass while Louis Armstrong's 'What A Wonderful World' played, with the audience responding with shocked silence.[64]

While these performances saw TISM gain a reputation as one of Australia's most dangerous live bands, it also served the dual purpose of unnerving any band who would play after them – effectively a concerted effort to say, 'How are you going to follow *that*?'

---

[62] Jeff Jenkins, 'Balaclava Road Warriors', *Inpress* 515, 8 July 1998, 9.
[63] Bob Hart, 'Humphrey', *The Herald Sun*, 21 September 2002, W-02.
[64] Butler and Kelly, 'RealiTISM', 14 April 2012.

2 The mystery of the artist explained

Oh tell me, why play rock 'n' roll? – 'Jesus Pots the White Ball' (1993)

Emboldened by the release of their debut album, TISM entered the studio with *Truckin' Songs'* engineer Clive Martin in May 1989 to record 'I Don't Want TISM I Want a Girlfriend' and 'I'll 'Ave Ya', which were released as a double A-side single[1] in December.

In 1990, the collapse of the independent Musicland label was preceded by TISM's own exit from the label, which saw them courted by majors such as CBS. While these negotiations would fail due to TISM's alleged demands for creative control, limited desire for press and self-described 'unmerited pomposity',[2] the band signed to local Polygram subsidiary Phonogram for an undisclosed sum.

What followed was the recording of the band's second album, *Hot Dogma*. Beginning in March 1990, the group recorded a number of demos with producers Malcolm Dennis, Peter Blyton and Laurence Maddy – the latter of whom

---

[1] A double A-side is a single featuring two tracks that are deemed as important as each other, and therefore sees no track being promoted over the other.
[2] TISM, *Collected Recordings 1986–1993* (sleeve notes, Genre B. Goode/Shock Records, 1995).

had previously performed alongside TISM as a member of Cattletruck.

The initial sessions in March were the first for Maddy, who would ultimately record the majority of *Machiavelli and the Four Seasons* with the group. Blyton had recommended Maddy venture into the world of production, with *Hot Dogma* seeing him join as keyboard programmer.

In August, the group published *The TISM Guide to Little Aesthetics*, their debut book which had been alluded to since 1986. A collection of lyrics, press releases and writings, its initial publication had been delayed due to the inclusion of names which had to be redacted for legal reasons. As a result, the majority of copies released were adorned with a sticker bearing the words 'Censored Due to Legal Advice', and the offending words covered with a mixture of black marker and correction fluid.

Upon *Hot Dogma*'s release on 1 October, critical reception was not quite as positive as its predecessor, with the record reaching a peak of #86 on the ARIA charts and garnering no reviews from publications such as *Rolling Stone*.

While the album was received well amongst fans and resulted in a tour that featured their first dates in Western Australia, amongst the band, *Hot Dogma* proved not only divisive but something of a turning point.

The record's release was hampered by a lack of promotion, and it became the final album to feature Van Vlalen, who chose to quit the band reportedly due to a growing dissatisfaction with the band's lack of musical evolution.[3] Purdy also parted

---

[3] Butler and Kelly, 'RealiTISM', 14 April 2012.

ways with the band, and in late 1991, the executive who signed TISM to Phonogram made his exit from the company:

> Despite their considerable financial input, Polygram's hopes of making TISM 'crossover' have failed, and amidst the atmosphere of confrontation and acrimony, the label, faced with further embarrassing pay outs to the band, takes the only sane option and sacks them.[4]

In November 1993, TISM made their disdain for the album known publicly, with a press release titled 'Hot Dogma: Re-issued and Reconsidered' simply referring to the album as 'dog's balls' and calling their decision to reissue the album a 'last, hopelessly doomed effort for the salvaging of its critical reputation'.[5]

Even by 1995, the band's tone had not lightened, with Hitler-Barassi calling it a 'waste of everyone's time' and Flaubert admitting, 'we weren't good enough artists to face the pressures of releasing a record when we were half popular'.[6]

Added Hitler-Barassi:

> [Hot Dogma is] quite possibly the worst record ever released by an alternative band in Australian recording history. There's nothing right about Hot Dogma. It's got that spurious underground self-righteousness combined with a poor

---

[4] TISM, *Collected Recordings*.
[5] TISM, 'Hot Dogma: Re-issued And Reconsidered', media release, 22 November 1993.
[6] Gavin Sawford, 'You're Only as Jung as You Feel', *Rave* 173, February 1995, 16.

attempt at slick, mainstream commerciality, and it gets neither right.[7]

Van Vlalen provided another recollection in 2024:

> For [*Truckin' Songs*] we didn't give a shit about the audience, we were just exploring. By the time we got to *Hot Dogma* we were consciously trying to recapture the best of [*Truckin' Songs*], the 'essence' of what had worked. For me, with *Hot Dogma*, we stopped exploring, instead we had become a 'cover band' of ourselves.[8]

The album would later be included as part of the band's *Collected Recordings 1986–1993* compilation in 1995, albeit trimmed down to a mere fourteen tracks from its original twenty-five, and complemented by a collection of the album's demos.

Recognizing a distinct need to refocus their efforts, TISM signed to Melbourne independent label Shock in late 1991 and debuted their new guitarist – Tony Coitus (later to be renamed Tokin' Blackman in 1995) – at a secret gig at Collingwood's Tote Hotel in January 1992. In March, the group entered the studio with famed producer Tony Cohen to record a new EP titled *The Beasts of Suburban*.

Cohen, who had previously worked with bands such as Beasts of Bourbon (whom the EP's title referenced), apparently

---

[7] Simon McKenzie, 'Begorrah! (Part One)', *Time Off*, 12 July 1995.
[8] Sean Anthony Kelly, 'I Reckon "Hot Dogma" Suffered from Three Things', Facebook, 7 June 2024. https://www.facebook.com/tismforever/posts/pfb id0ChuQULyhJom2EEivr6Vvvu9VqAvWaTwPywceBarxPP859ux6nMmwndrdq CdLxKnCl?comment_id=474434048494892.

flew back from working with Nick Cave in California to facilitate the sessions.[9] Musically, the record was in line with what fans may have expected from a collaboration with TISM and Cohen, though Hitler-Barassi would later label it a 'mish-mash of Oz-rock cliches and reverb twin-guitar attack'.[10]

Released in July 1992 and eschewing much of the already-dated sound of *Hot Dogma*, the eight-track record was more in line with their vision for the future. Gone were the distinctly 1980s sounds of their second album, and instead, their newest effort combined elements of accessible guitar-heavy pop rock and – most notably – their first foray into actual sampling.

In a way, the EP had its foot in two worlds. On the one hand, the group were looking to continue evolving past what they had delivered with *Hot Dogma*, yet on the other, the introduction of an accomplished guitarist such as Blackman meant they wanted to ensure he felt comfortable within his new role.

In his posthumous memoir, Cohen recalled that the pre-production meeting of the album left him unsure how to perceive the band, though their work and shared vision was impressive:

> TISM made me laugh. They were really well organised. Perhaps too well organised compared with other musicians I'd met.[11]

---

[9] TISM, *Collected Recordings*.
[10] McKenzie, "'Begorrah!'".
[11] Tony Cohen and John Olson, *Half Deaf, Completely Mad* (Melbourne: Black Inc., 2023), 166.

Describing the band as 'very professional', Cohen's efforts were recognized with a nomination at the 1993 ARIA Awards, receiving a nod for Producer of the Year for his work on both *The Beasts of Suburban* and The Cruel Sea's *This Is Not the Way Home*, while the record itself was also nominated for Best Independent Release.

Despite his reportedly positive relationship with TISM, the band immortalized Cohen's presence by having him record a satirical critique they included at the end of the EP:

> TISM lacks the sheer guts of anything like, say, the Beasts of Bourbon. I mean, there's a gutsy band. Of course their cheap sarcasm, it pretty well doesn't get there. It's not real good. It doesn't approach the epic sort of comedy and wit of The Birthday Party.

Perhaps emboldened by the more positive reception to their latest effort, TISM began plans for their next release in late 1992. Once again working with Maddy, a handful of songs were recorded at Platinum Studios, including 'Australia – The World's Suburb', 'Consumption Tax' and 'The Ballad of Paul Keating',[12] which would not be released until their inclusion on the *Collected Recordings* compilation. Another song, titled

---

[12] Paul Keating had previously served as treasurer of Australia under Prime Minister Bob Hawke from 1983 to 1991, deputy prime minister of Australia from 1990 to 1991 and prime minister of Australia from 1991 to 1996. During his tenure as treasurer in 1983, TISM penned letters inviting Keating – along with American novelist Philip Roth and guitarist Eddie Van Halen – to join the band as lead tambourinist. Two members of the Federal Police responded on Keating's behalf.

'The Last Soviet Star', was also recorded during these sessions and would not see an official release until 2023.

In July 1993, TISM again entered the studio with Cohen to record new material. In his memoir, Cohen recalled that 'someone else'[13] had remixed his efforts on the resulting EP, with TISM reportedly asserting he had made the band 'sound too nasty'.[14] These sessions would be issued on 3 September as a EP titled *Australia the Lucky Cunt*.[15]

Featuring only four songs recorded in the studio and one diatribe recorded at the band's appearance at the Melbourne Big Day Out[16] in January that year, the EP was in the same vein as *The Beasts of Suburban* and featured a more focused approach to hard rock. Hitler-Barassi would later reflect on the EP, labelling it 'a really shoddy, ill-conceived and poorly-recorded record'.[17]

The EP almost went unheard, however, thanks to a larger battle around its artwork that quickly overshadowed the release. Adorned with the band's name, the cover featured an image of the sun and a koala with a hypodermic needle placed in its mouth, all designed in a style allegedly reminiscent of artist Ken Done.[18]

---

[13] Ibid.
[14] Ibid.
[15] Despite its official title, ARIA referred to the EP as *Lose Your Delusions*.
[16] The Big Day Out was an influential annual touring festival which ran from 1992 to 1997 and 1999 to 2014, with local and international bands performing across Australia and New Zealand.
[17] McKenzie, 'Begorrah!'.
[18] Ken Done is a Sydney artist and designer whose vibrant work, overtly Australian subject matter, and recognizable style can equally be found in both art galleries and souvenir stores.

A week after the record's release, both Shock Records and TISM management received letters from Done's managing director demanding all physical copies of the EP and its promotional materials be withdrawn and destroyed, along with the payment of damages 'for breach of copyright and distress'.[19]

By 25 September, all copies of the EP were withdrawn from sale, and negotiations had begun about 'damages done to Done's reputation as an artist',[20] and internal discussions commenced regarding new artwork for a reissue. Mockups were made which altered the offending artwork with silver foil before a new version – now retitled *Censored Due to Legal Advice* – was issued on 25 October. The reissue's artwork depicted Sinéad O'Connor's 1992 appearance on *Saturday Night Live*, in which she tore up a picture of Pope John Paul II, with the Pope's image altered to read 'TISM' instead.

Recalled Shock's David Williams:

There was certainly an element of the Barbra Streisand effect, which Ken Done's people hadn't really anticipated. triple j didn't want to play anything off that EP, so it would have just disappeared very quickly. Instead, it became notorious.[21]

As the cover controversy was unfolding, TISM found themselves back in the studio working on new material.

---

[19] TISM, 'TISM and Ken Done: A Timeline', media release, October 1993.
[20] Ibid.
[21] Unless otherwise accredited, all quotes are from interviews with the author (Thrussell, 20 January 2024; McKercher, 22 January 2024; Maddy, 19 February 2024; Martin, 2 May 2024; Williams, 27 May 2024).

This time, the sessions were with engineer and former triple j live music producer Paul McKercher at Metropolis Studios, and bore three songs: 'Jung Talent Time', 'Aussiemandias' and 'State Schools Are Great Schools'. While the former two would later appear on *Machiavelli*, the latter would not be released until late 1995 on TISM's *Collected Recordings* compilation.

As McKercher recalls of the experience, his reputation as a 'solid engineer who could capture the nuance of sound well' was likely the reason for TISM's decision to work with him:

> I sensed that they didn't need or want a producer involving themselves in rewriting or imposing their tastes too much. Rather, they knew what they sounded like and wanted someone to capture it competently.

Describing the band as 'a sweet bunch' who were 'warm, charming, conversational, and genuinely enthused about the process of recording', McKercher's experience with TISM was in stark contrast to the public image they had made for themselves. These sessions did not, however, result in discussions of what had come before:

> Perhaps this was part of the band's propelling themselves towards a different overall sound. The crunchy metal guitars remained, but now overlaid with oddly hilarious techno beats and house pianos. I may have misjudged this at the time, but it seemed that the music component was more so a vehicle for their biting satire and something that would be fun to play and for the crowds to mosh to, rather than a study in complex harmonic movement.

3 Machiavelli and the Four Seasons

And so, I warn you Aussie youth, rock and roll is full of lies; don't be like your rock heroes, or you'll have normal happy lives. – 'Backstage with Ron Hitler' (1998)

Likely tired by the legal controversy which had marred the final quarter of the previous year, TISM began 1994 by performing at the Gold Coast, Sydney and Adelaide legs of the national Big Day Out festival, whose bill featured Soundgarden, the Smashing Pumpkins and the Ramones.

As Flaubert would later explain, the group's slot on the festival's line-up reminded them of their roots. With TISM's early days featuring 'cheap, tacky little drum machines',[1] their growth and success resulted in them meeting more professionals within the music industry. This departure from the initial DIY aesthetic of their earliest bedroom incarnation into more polished surroundings was cited as the reason for *Hot Dogma*'s derision within the group.

'You get subsumed into the great thing of rock, [and] we sort of lost our way', Flaubert said. 'And I think that's the trouble

---
[1] Sawford, 'You're Only As Jung', 17.

with *Hot Dogma*, it sounds at last like a real rock album by a real band.'[2]

The Big Day Out tour saw Flaubert and Hitler-Barassi venturing away from the heavier alternative-rock and grunge of the main stage and towards the electronic sounds of the festival's Boiler Room stage which featured Australian house outfit Southend at the Gold Coast and Sydney legs of the festival. 'They're not like the greatest band out or anything, but we both looked at each other and said "This is what we used to sound like and let's go back jolly well and do it"', said Flaubert.

The liner notes for *Machiavelli* see the band cite this musical revelation as the reason they abandoned the 'first version' of the album they had already recorded 'on the sort of careless whim that makes TISM the insouciant dilettantes they are'.[3] This version simply included the tracks they had recorded with Maddy in 1992 and McKercher in 1993. A more cynical account of their musical awakening was offered by Hitler-Barassi, who claimed the decision was made for far more superficial reasons:

> When you go to the Big Day Out on the main stage there's Soundgarden or Ministry and you know it's full of blokes shaking their heads like a scene from *Wayne's World 2* and you go up to the techno room and there's all these girls dancing having fun showing their navels. That bloody clinched it for us.[4]

---

[2] Ibid.
[3] TISM, *Machiavelli and the Four Seasons* (sleeve notes, Genre B. Goode/Shock Records, 1995).
[4] Sawford, 'You're Only As Jung', 17.

Indeed, the refreshing change in style appears to have been a welcome one for TISM, who, in the midst of the grunge explosion of the early 1990s, were growing tired of the ubiquitous music trends. Guitar music was later noted as something that TISM were 'slightly opposed to in that era',[5] with the likes of Flaubert eagerly looking towards other musicians whom he regarded as boundary-pushing.

Origins of the band's shift in technology could be traced back to performances with Pop Will Eat Itself, or how other UK names such as Carter USM began to fuse dance music and technology, but TISM first began taking baby steps towards that very sound on *The Beasts of Suburban*. In contrast to the most conservative rock sound of *Hot Dogma*, their 1992 release saw the band beginning to stretch their legs, with tracks such as 'Get Thee to a Nunnery' and 'Lillee Caught Dilley Bowled Milli Vanilli' showing what could be deemed the future sound of TISM.[6]

By 1993, TISM's performances with Caligula had exposed the group to another example of musicians experimenting with heavy sampling and loop-based compositions, and by the time the band hit the stage for their Big Day Out appearance, their live set had expanded to contain an ADAT (Alesis Digital Audio Tape) to aid in the delivery of samples on stage.

Recalled Williams:

I see the progression from the start of the *Beasts* sessions all the way to when they'd finished up with *Machiavelli*. For me,

---
[5] Damian Cowell, Interview with Zan Rowe, *Take 5*. Double J, 14 September 2018.
[6] Not to be confused with The DC3's 2011 album, *The Future Sound of Nostalgia*.

that's a real bookended period. Post-*Machiavelli* was probably even a bigger change, just in the way that they worked. They started with a fresh batch of ideas, whereas some of *Machiavelli* were ideas or lyrics that they'd been working on for a while, and they finally found a way to deliver them in a way that they were happy with. But it was a culmination of three-to-four years of work.

Part of their contemporary sonic evolution came from a trip to London in 1993, during which they discovered and purchased a number of sample CDs that allowed them to continue expanding their sound both in the studio and on the live stage via an E-mu Emax sampler.

While de la Hot-Croix Bun was often at the forefront of technology within the band due to the myriad technological advancements for keyboard, Flaubert notes the discovery of 'intelligent dance music'[7] by way of New Order's post-punk sensibilities and their electronic instrumentation was what inspired him to first purchase a Roland TR-606 Drumatix drum machine from Ringwood's Hans Music Spot. 'From that moment on, the lure of the dance beat was never far away from me', he would claim.[8]

For others in the band, groups like Severed Heads, or the sample-heavy *My Life in the Bush of Ghosts* album from Brian Eno and David Byrne were influential in terms of how they approached electronic music. TISM were never far away from

---

[7] Damian Cowell, 'Episode 15: Remember Nostalgia?', *Only the Shit You Love: The Podcast*, 3 November 2021. https://podcasts.apple.com/au/podcast/podcast-14-episode-15-remember-nostalgia/id1585650286?i=1000540575905.
[8] Ibid.

artificial instrumentation though. After all, their pioneering use of drum machines in the 1980s as a 'tacky disco band'[9] would set them apart from the bands who lugged around full kits.

According to Hitler-Barassi:

What we feel we've done now is return to our roots, and our roots have always been very machine-oriented and very mechanical. We've always had a drum machine, the tackier the better and we've always had keyboard lines and the cornier the better. We were techno before because we weren't good enough to be anything else. We needed a Casio beat, we needed a drum machine. We couldn't pull it off without a lot of mechanical assistance.[10]

Starting with their TR-606, the group's collection of instruments grew over the years. Flaubert would also utilize Roland's TR-808 and TR-909 models, and an Alesis D4 drum module alongside Yamaha DX7 and DX11 synthesizers. Meanwhile, his sampling would also be achieved via an Akai S2800 with increased memory, Cubase software, Alesis and Fostex 8-track ADAT machines, and Roland D-550 and TB-303 bass synths.[11] For de la Hot-Croix Bun, his equipment would include the use of a Roland JV-1080 digital module and a Casio MT-68, though it was the long-standing 1980 Korg PolySix analog synth with MIDI conversion which would be his synthesizer of choice.[12]

---
[9] Humphrey B. Flaubert, *The J Files*, triple j, 28 March 1996.
[10] Buttfield, 'Crusaders'.
[11] TISM, 'Who Are TISM?', *TISM*. http://www.tism.com.au/whoaretism/frames.html, archived 6 December 2000, at the Wayback Machine.
[12] Ibid.

For Flaubert, it was the early 1990s when he began properly indoctrinating himself into the world of dance music. Alongside the band's growing live and studio setup, and the exposure to what opportunities technology could provide for the band, his weekends were spent listening to 3RRR's electronic music programme *Tranzmission*, which saw presenter Kate Bathgate highlight artists such as German trance artist Cosmic Baby, who resonated with Flaubert.[13]

It was this that would lead TISM into a full-fledged love affair with the 'fluffy disco-pop tinsel-packaged drivel'[14] which would make up their next record. Having intended *Australia the Lucky Cunt* as a pre-album teaser for their next full length album, a 1995 press release claimed that TISM 'experienced an all-too rare moment of conscience, and scrapped the project before it reached the unsuspecting public's ears'.[15]

The press release claimed TISM felt they were 'losing their way, re-visiting their roots and seeking to become in touch with themselves'.[16] As a result, they 'returned to their bedrooms to toss off a fresh collection of rubbish'[17] in January 1994, before a fictitious computer virus 'acting on behalf of good taste everywhere'[18] reportedly destroyed what they had created thus far.

Unlike their earliest work, *Machiavelli* didn't see the band working together quite as closely as was preferred. With de

---
[13] Cowell, *Only the Shit You Love*, 3 November 2021.
[14] TISM, '*T.I.S.M. – Why??*'.
[15] Ibid.
[16] Ibid.
[17] TISM, *Machiavelli and the Four Seasons*.
[18] Ibid.

la Hot-Croix Bun often occupied with commitments outside of Melbourne and Flaubert embracing the ability to create remotely, other members of the group would get together for 'slam 'em down sessions' in which ideas were recorded, before tapes were sent to Flaubert who would track drums and add samples.

In August, TISM returned to the stage to play their first shows – all unannounced secret gigs – since their transformative Big Day Out appearances, with the band billed under pseudonyms such as Machiavelli and the Four Seasons, The Frank Vitkovic Jazz Experience[19] and Late for Breakfast.

Between these secret dates, TISM would take five days in September to visit Melbourne's Platinum Studios to record the remainder of their forthcoming album with Maddy. These same sessions also resulted in the tracks which would be issued as B-sides.

Having worked with Maddy on *Hot Dogma* and on a handful of tracks in late 1992, Maddy would later suggest that the reason for their return to him as producer was largely due to the professional association they had created.

'I think it was purely the relationship in the studio and the productive way in which we worked', he recalled. 'I was very sympathetic to where they wanted to go; understanding was a big part of it.'

Maddy continued:

---

[19] One of the three shows under this name saw TISM billed as The Frank Vitkovic Jazz Quartet.

> I can't profess to fully understand TISM – I'm not sure anybody can – but I was sympathetic to what they were doing and the fact that they had specific things they wanted to do. They make some interesting calls from a producer's point of view of wanting to leave things that I would maybe change under normal circumstances, and vice versa, but I was willing to go with them on that.

Despite having sat in the producer's chair, Maddy himself didn't particularly recognize the work being done for this new album as having been entirely different to what had come before:

> I've read before about them shifting from this rock sound, but I don't know that I really see that. I always saw that electronica thing in there, and I think it's mainly because of Humphrey's drum programming. It's just got this machine-like sound about it and I think that's scattered all through *Hot Dogma* as well.

* * *

On 13 February 1995, TISM broke their musical silence with the release of their first piece of new music in almost eighteen months. Dubbed 'Jung Talent Time', the single's release was curious, given it featured eight identically named tracks which were different remixes of the song by David Thrussell and Pieter Bourke of 'industrial-techno-experimental'[20] outfit Snog.

---

[20] TISM, *T.I.S.M. – Why??.*

A stark contrast to what had come before, the 'press release bullshit'[21] which announced its release noted that the single showed 'a new direction'[22] for the band's music. 'We got other people to write, arrange, record and produce it', Flaubert claimed. 'David Thrussell from Snog did this one. We feel this is a great leap forward in the band's artistic life.'[23]

The same press release also teased news of a new album set for release around March or April, though Flaubert continued in the same vein, claiming not to have heard the new record:

> We believe in following our artistic principles most strictly. And given our new beliefs in total artistic lack of input, we thought we'd keep right out of it. You know, one of our suggestions might have filtered in there in the studio and wrecked the whole thing.[24]

Ironically, the new single actually saw TISM going all-in with their own involvement, given the CD was the first released under their nascent Genre B. Goode record label. Distributed by Shock, the label was a nod to the band's own roots, being named after their founding member of the same name, though early plans included naming it 'Pollygram' in reference to their former label.[25]

Following a nine-date run around the country as part of the 90210-Week Tour in February and March, TISM slowly eased

---

[21] Sawford, 'You're Only As Jung', 16.
[22] TISM, 'New Single and Album to Be Released Soon', media release, February 1995.
[23] Ibid.
[24] Ibid.
[25] Cowell, 'The Birth of Uncool'.

themselves into promotional efforts for their upcoming album. With promotional copies of the record finding their way out to the media throughout April, so too did triple j begin broadcasting the band's next single, '(He'll Never Be An) Ol' Man River'. The band would also make an appearance on community television station C31 Melbourne's weekly variety programme *Under Melbourne Tonight* on 27 April, performing the aforementioned track along with the still-unreleased 'Protest Song'.

On 4 May 1995, TISM officially released *Machiavelli and the Four Seasons* into the world. The album was initially issued on both compact disc and cassette; however, for those wishing to find a copy of the record in stores, TISM had purposely made the entire process far more difficult than necessary.

One of *Machiavelli*'s most notable aspects was the non-commercial artwork it was packaged with. Notably, its outer artwork is wholly absent of any mention of TISM whatsoever. It wasn't until the record's 2023 issue that the name TISM appeared anywhere on the package at all – albeit relegated to the spine.

Stickers were eventually attached to the record asserting that 'this is actually a TISM album', ostensibly at the request of Shock, who presumably realized that an album which was hard to find in stores would be unlikely to sell well.

This was largely due in part to the image that adorned the outer sleeve, which was a direct appropriation of the self-titled 1960 release by American ensemble The Hollywood Argyles – a vocal group largely remembered for their chart-topping debut single, 'Alley Oop'.

Formed by Gary S. Paxton (who would later gain fame as the producer of 'Monster Mash' by Bobby 'Boris' Pickett and the Crypt-Kickers) and Kim Fowley (who would later manage The Runaways), The Hollywood Argyles were a largely studio-based ensemble based around Paxton's efforts.

Machiavelli's artwork therefore features Paxton front and centre in a grey suit, surrounded by Little Bobby Rey, Ted Marsh, Gary 'Spider' Webb, Ted Winters and Derry Weaver, who had all served as session musicians on the original record.[26]

Though likely unintended, there's a slight irony about TISM using the cover of their album to present themselves as a fake band given that Paxton would assert that apart from himself, 'there were no actual Hollywood Argyles'.[27]

The Hollywood Argyles entered TISM's world when Flaubert found a copy of the album at a second-hand record store in the eastern Melbourne suburb of Burwood. Amused by the artwork and the fact the band seemed to be the very epitome of 'uncool', the image was paired with the title of an unreleased song from *The Beasts of Suburban* era called 'Machiavelli and the Four Seasons'.

Written by Hitler-Barassi, the song's title paired both assonance and reference of New Jersey doo-wop band Frankie Valli and the Four Seasons with that of the sixteenth-century Florentine diplomat Niccolò Machiavelli, whose work within the fields of political philosophy and science has resulted

---
[26] Michael Jack Kirby, 'Hollywood Argyles', *Way Back Attack*, Accessed 16 November 2023. https://www.waybackattack.com/hollywoodargyles.html.
[27] Jerry Osborne, 'The Checkered Past of the Hollywood Argyles', *Tampa Bay Times*, 18 April 1997. https://www.tampabay.com/archive/1997/04/18/the-checkered-past-of-the-hollywood-argyles/.

in his name having 'long stood for all that is deep, dark, and treacherous in political leadership'.[28]

A continuation of the melding of culture seen within the members' pseudonyms, this contradiction of saccharine pop and stern politics combined to present the record as the latest release from a fictional band – one TISM's fan base was unlikely to stumble upon.

Connections could also be made to Frank Zappa and The Mothers of Invention's 1968 album, *Cruising with Ruben & the Jets*. Released under the titular alias, the record was made as a parody of the doo-wop genre and featured The Mothers as illustrated anthropomorphic dogs on the cover. The only reference to the real band was featured in a speech bubble on the cover which asked, 'Is this the Mothers of Invention recording under a different name in a last ditch attempt to get their cruddy music on the radio?'

As Williams recalled:

> The concept was that they would have this outer cover and no one would know what it was, and then there was the inner cover, which was the 'real' cover. The booklet that came inside the case was the techno-inspired cover which was supposed to go with the flavour of particular music by being computer designed.

The deceit continued on the album's rear, which featured an essay from then-manager Michael Lynch containing

---

[28] Michael Lynch, *Machiavelli and the Four Seasons* (sleeve notes, Genre B. Goode/Shock Records, 1995).

biographies of both the fictional band and their historical namesake.

Per the biography, the group were said to hail from the fictitious town of Springvale, Maine (named for the band's own home suburb), where their long hair and unique vocal sound – including 'the melismatic trilling of the lead vocal, those angelic four part harmonies' – had resulted in Lynch discovering them in a 'crowded, sweaty underground club in Springvale', and resulting in their signing to the Genre B. Goode Records label:

> Now that Elvis is in the army, I confidently predict that this will be the new thing for 1963,[29] and once you listen to this album, you'll be convinced too. The charts are calling out for a new group to take the world by storm – and here it is – Machiavelli and the Four Seasons. I'm prepared to stake my record company on it.[30]

In keeping with the theme, the rear artwork presented a false tracklist mocking the perceived homogenous nature of most doo-wop songs of the era:

Side One:

1. 'I Love You Baby'
2. 'You And Me, Baby Love'
3. 'Baby I Love You'
4. 'Love; Baby-You'
5. 'Its You I Love, Baby'

---

[29] Elvis Presley's military service had actually ended three years earlier, in 1960.
[30] Lynch, *Machiavelli and the Four Seasons*.

Side Two:

1. 'In Love With You, Baby'
2. 'Baby, Baby, Baby'
3. 'Love, Love, Love'
4. 'Baby Love'
5. 'I.L.Y.B.'

Those able to see past the confounding artwork were then faced by a second problem relating to the very package itself. The initial CD edition of the album was sold in a small cardboard box housed in a brittle plastic shell, which broke easily.

Initially, the plan was for the record to be issued with a flip-top cover to showcase the inner and outer artwork. The easiest method was to package the record as a Digipak – something traditionally viewed by retailers as being associated with singles or EPs, though, would later become a standard form for albums. With vendors preferring jewel cases, a compromise was struck by providing an open-at-the-top, moulded plastic case, as Williams recalled:

> The plastic moulding company delivered us these cases, which we had to pop together and then put the cardboard box into the case – which was great, except the moment that they started going into retail, the fucking things fell apart.

After selling a couple thousand copies of the moulded cases, the swift second pressing of the album was housed in a standard CD jewel case, though the confusing artwork remained. The inner artwork was more straightforward, featuring the band's then-logo atop a series of computer-generated graphics. The logo was circled with the words 'London, New York, Berlin, Springvale' – satirically positioning the band's home suburb of Springvale as one of the world's most fashionable cities.

As the first TISM comic book asserted in late May 1995, behind the intriguing cover was a new musical exploration for the band, with Flaubert claiming their foray into techno was 'the best thing we ever did'.[31] Elsewhere, the comic claimed the album 'represents a turning point for the band – they became listenable'.[32]

In interviews, however, Flaubert aimed to downplay expectations:

> The general vibe on this record is plastic, plug it in. We're a bit of a dance band and hopefully people will sit up and take notice. It's not going to change the course of modern-day music but you never can tell.[33]

'(He'll Never Be An) Ol' Man River'

For those unaware of TISM prior to 1995, the song which likely introduced them to the band was the album's second single, '(He'll Never Be An) Ol' Man River'. What became their biggest commercial success took inspiration from an event which

---

[31] Mark Sexton and John Petropoulos, *TISM #1* (Melbourne: AAARGH! Comics, 1995), 15.
[32] Ibid.
[33] Sash Crocostimpy, 'Is This Serious, Mum?', *Rip It Up* 308, 9 March 1995, 50.

occurred during the group's most stressful period. One week after the band reissued their previous EP as *Censored Due to Legal Advice*, on 31 October 1993, the American actor River Phoenix passed away at the age of twenty-three from a drug overdose of cocaine and heroin after collapsing at Californian nightspot The Viper Room.

At the band's first performance since Phoenix's passing – at the all-ages Pushover festival at Melbourne's Olympic Park on 20 November – Hitler-Barassi performed a diatribe before the largely teenage crowd. Alongside lines namechecking the likes of soap operas such as the American *Beverly Hills, 90210* and the Australian *Neighbours*, Hitler-Barassi asserted, 'Everyone here is surely agreed, it was fucking great River Phoenix OD'd'.[34]

The song was initially inspired by an acquaintance uttering the opening line to Hitler-Barassi, which then gave rise to its eventual title, which paired a reference to the late actor with 'Ol' Man River', a show tune composed by Jerome Kern with lyrics by Oscar Hammerstein II for the 1927 musical *Show Boat*.

Though the track has long been condemned as being a cheap shot at Phoenix's passing, a closer look discovers a focus on celebrity worship and the deconstruction of fame itself. In TISM's own press release, they describe it as a 'song of admiration' and 'praise' about 'celebrating the people who went that little bit further'.[35]

Alongside Phoenix's passing, it namechecks a number of other famous individuals, including Sir Edmund Hillary and

---

[34] TISM, 'TISM's Occasional Pieces', media release, March 1994.
[35] TISM, 'I'm on the Drug That Killed River Phoenix', media release, 5 June 1995.

Neil Armstrong, the first men to scale Mount Everest and land on the moon, respectively.

Elsewhere, celebrity death is again a topic of conversation, looking at the infamous passings of AC/DC frontman Bon Scott, famed guitarist Jimi Hendrix, members of rock outfit Lynyrd Skynyrd and 'Mama' Cass Elliot of The Mamas & The Papas.[36]

The track also references singer Michael Jackson, predicting he would be the next drug-related death to occur. Jackson wouldn't pass away until 2009, though the prediction wasn't unfounded, with his death being attributed to acute propofol (an anesthetic and sedative) intoxication.

An early demo of the song indicates it was largely built around a twin-guitar attack from Blackman and Cheese at first, before the elements of synthesizer and techno drums were later added along with a synth bassline. While the song lyrically stayed largely the same between demos, the earliest version does see the line 'I'm on the drug' changed to 'he's on the drug' and 'we're on the drug', perhaps implying that celebrity worship is a communal experience and avoiding any apparent self-incrimination.

Initially released to radio in April, the track's sudden popularity upon the album's May release resulted in the swift production of a CD single to be issued in June.[37] The accompanying artwork depicted a tombstone complete with

---

[36] The lyrics refer to the urban legend Mama Cass died from choking on a ham sandwich, though her official cause of death was a heart attack.
[37] MTV News Staff, 'Australian Band "On The Drug That Killed River Phoenix"', *MTV*, 7 June 1995. http://www.mtv.com/news/504382/australian-band-on-the-drug-that-killed-river-phoenix/.

Phoenix's birth and death date, the band's name and the song's full title. Shortly after its release, another version of the single was manufactured. Released in greater numbers, this edition featured an image of assorted pills and – most importantly – the song's opening lyrics.

Though rumours circulated the initial CD single was pulled from shelves due to controversy, the truth was that the second version of the artwork featured the song's most prominent line, thus making it easier for consumers to find, as Williams recalls:

> By calling something '(He'll Never Be An) Ol' Man River', when someone walks into a record store and says, 'I want that song, "I'm on the Drug That Killed River Phoenix"', there's going to be a disconnect. It might have been an issue for *Australia the Lucky Cunt*, too. People might have found it difficult to find the lead song which also had a misleading title, but it wasn't really a problem for that LP because no one wanted it.

However, real controversy for the track wasn't far behind, with the band largely chastised for mocking a celebrity whose death was still fresh in the mind of the general public. As with most press engagements, TISM would straddle the line between fact and fiction in terms of their responses.

In 2004, Hitler-Barassi asserted that the track 'wasn't about River Phoenix at all', claiming 'that song was about fame, and the people listed in it weren't even real celebrities'.[38] Flaubert

---

[38] Michael Dwyer, 'The Phantom Menace', *The Age EG*, 2 July 2004. https://www.theage.com.au/entertainment/music/the-phantom-menace-20040702-gdy5ls.html.

had previously labelled it 'our awful revenge upon the successful people of the world'.[39]

'[River] had lots of things. He had talent, he had money, he had success, he was good looking, he was, in all ways, what we weren't and we just wanted to drag him down to our level', added Hitler-Barassi. 'He is in the Viper Room of life but we're continually on the pavement outside it.'[40]

One of the band's biggest controversies occurred in 1996 when Red Hot Chili Peppers' bassist Flea – who rode in the ambulance with Phoenix on the night he passed away – commented on the song.

On 4 May, Flea – who had been born in Melbourne and owned property on the south coast of New South Wales – visited triple j's Sydney studios to speak to host Francis Leach for the station's Hi-5 segment. Breaking away from discussing Fela Kuti's 'Gentleman' to address Leach's question about music as comfort, Flea recalled hearing '(He'll Never Be An) Ol' Man River' in an uncharacteristically unguarded series of comments:

> I heard a song that offended me greatly on triple j. I nearly wanted to smash my radio with a hammer and drive down to triple j and kill the DJ, and then find the band and kill them. And it was a song by a band – I found out they're called TISM, and . . . I don't even want to talk about it [. . .] I'm not really a violent person but my first instinct was to smash their faces in.[41]

---

[39] Leonard P. Coaltrain, 'TISM Unmasked – Rock'n'Roll Whoppers without the Green Bits', *Revelation* 14, August 1995, 15.
[40] Ibid.
[41] Flea, Interview with Francis Leach, *Hi-5*. triple j, 4 May 1996.

TISM would only directly respond to the incident a few times over the years, including the following month, when Hitler-Barassi said, 'I really do hope that he beats my head in 'cause it'd be the closest I've ever been to a real rock star'.[42]

In 2004, Hitler-Barassi addressed the incident by recollecting a fictitious encounter with Flea:

> I had him on the ground and I was just about to break his nose with my forehead and I said, 'You do know, Flea, that satire is a legitimate art form stretching back to ancient Greek drama?' And he said, 'Oh, that's OK then, Ron'. He's a good guy, Flea. He's a mate of ours.[43]

Though Flea hasn't commented publicly on the song since, former triple j music director Richard Kingsmill once recalled that the bassist had mentioned the song to him before a 1999 interview, though their interaction wasn't recorded.[44]

TISM would, however, issue a satirical apology to Flea as part of a promotional video ahead of their 1996 UK tour,[45] while Flaubert would also express some half-hearted regret to both Phoenix and the Red Hot Chili Peppers in 2015.[46]

---

[42] Buttfield, 'The Hitler Diaries'.
[43] Dwyer, 'The Phantom Menace'.
[44] Richard Kingsmill, 'King Hit – Red Hot Chili Peppers', *triple j*. https://www.abc.net.au/triplej/media/s2306448.htm, archived 21 November 2012, at the Wayback Machine.
[45] Mark Bakaitis, 'TISM – UK Tour Promo (1996)', YouTube, 7 April 2014. https://www.youtube.com/watch?v=ew8GTsrsxHI.
[46] Zwar, 'TISM'S Damian Cowell'.

In 2022, a new diatribe entitled 'Old Skool TISM'[47] would close their performances and address the controversy, opening with the line: 'That River Phoenix song was wrong but I am gonna sing it strong, pretend my conscience still too young to know the harm I may have done.'

Despite (or perhaps because of) the controversy, the track would become the group's best performing single commercially. On the ARIA charts, it would peak at #23 in the week ending 25 June 1995, and in January 1996, it would hit #9 on triple j's annual Hottest 100 countdown – one position higher than their next single, 'Greg! The Stop Sign!!'.

'All Homeboys Are Dickheads'

In the narrative of *Machiavelli*'s tracklist, 'All Homeboys Are Dickheads' is the first to offer fans an insight into the more sample-heavy approach that TISM adopted for their new record.

In opposition to the almost kaleidoscopic sampling approach bands such as Pop Will Eat Itself took in their work, the vast majority of this track sees TISM lifting directly from The Johnny Otis Show's 1968 single 'Country Girl'.

Beginning with a simple repetitive drum loop, a warm synth pad accompanies the paired vocals of Flaubert and Cheese as they begin to expound upon a shared disdain for 'homeboys'

---

[47] 'Old Skool TISM' would later appear in their 2024 sets as an actual song, which would later be included on their *Death to Art* album that same year.

– that is, someone closely associated with a youth gang, often characterized by 'a baseball cap and a love of rap'.

As the first verse ends, the track shifts into a pair of samples from 'Country Girl'. Sampling the instrumental backing, the word 'wide' is repurposed to be heard as 'why',[48] while the ending sample of 'great big cunt' is actually an excised version of 'great big country girl'. Likewise, what sounds like a sampled violin solo is actually a portion of a guitar solo. The ending of the track is also notable within the context of the record as being one of the only songs – along with 'Play Mistral for Me' – to feature live drums from Flaubert.

Musical content notwithstanding, the track is emblematic of TISM's approach to youth culture of the era, though Flaubert asserted the track was not a direct attack on homeboys at all.[49] Their 1992 video *Boyz 'N the Hoods* captured the group performing at St Kilda venue The Palace on 4 September, dressed in oversized baseball caps and uniforms, seemingly mocking the stereotypical attire of the homeboy.

The topic was one addressed in their media interviews at the time. Hitler-Barassi ruminated on the topic in a 1995 interview, seemingly dismissing any particular outwardly negative aspects on homeboys, and instead criticized their lack of individuality – going so far as to compare group loyalty, shared language and use of a uniform to that of the police force:

---

[48] UK producer A Guy Called Gerald's 1988 debut single, 'Voodoo Ray', featured a similar sampling technique, excising the end of Peter Cook saying 'voodoo rage' to give the track its titular sample.
[49] Cowell, 'The Birth of Uncool'.

> The faults of being in a homie gang isn't one of being antisocial, being rebellious, being violent. I find that being in a homie gang, the faults there [are] you're too conservative, you're too reactionary, you're too standard, you're too normal.[50]

Some of the disdain also appears to be directed at the imitation of African American culture by Australian youths, who borrow heavily from hip-hop bands without appreciating context. This topic comes up in later song 'Play Mistral for Me', in which TISM touch on the confounding phenomenon of 'the racist kids who love Public Enemy'.

The band had also touched on it during their aforementioned performance at The Palace, when Hitler-Barassi performed a diatribe titled '"Don't Believe the Hype" Is Hype' (which also appears on the bonus disc of *Machiavelli*):

> Every crew member I've ever met seems to be turd, how come it's the illiterate that know every rapper's words? Up behind the shelter sheds black consciousness goes wrong – Malcolm X, he's from Run-DMC; Martin Luther King, from a U2 song.

A 1995 piece in the short-lived *Underworld* zine titled 'TISM's Reasons to Support American TV' underlined this notion further, with the band's tongue-in-cheek takedown of US television permeating the Australian market being punctuated with the line; 'Stop dissin' me, brother, coz one more American racks any

---
[50] Kieran Butler, 'Talcott (3CR) & Ron Hitler Barassi (TISM) 1995', YouTube, 29 August 2016. https://www.youtube.com/watch?v=1QGo0CutT0k.

more Australian culture, and we're gonna waste 'em'.[51] Even more direct, however, was their 1997 song 'Yob', which lists behaviour worthy of falling under the titular category, simply noting, 'if it's American, ape'.

Ultimately, though, the line 'a baseball cap and a love of rap might need sympathy, but still, possibly a homeboy could be a dickhead pure and simple' seems to indicate that homeboys are but an easy hook for the song, with titular dickheads existing regardless of their attire.

Also of note is the reference to Fyodor Dostoevsky's 1879 novel *The Brothers Karamazov*, which itself serves to contrast the lower-class homeboys with revered literature. Previously focused on in *The TISM Guide to Little Aesthetics*,[52] a satirical Q&A session with *Hot Metal*, an Australian magazine about heavy metal, also referenced Dostoevsky's work, with the TISM-penned questions ostensibly serving as a summation of the band's own view of their craft:

> When you quote Dostoyevsky and Christ are you showing your literate selves or being lazy, over-dramatic little attention grabbers like Nick Cave?[53]

---

[51] TISM, 'TISM's Reasons to Support American TV', *Underworld* 3, December 1995, 35.
[52] TISM, *The TISM Guide to Little Aesthetics*, 147.
[53] TISM, 'TISM Meets Hot Metal', *Hot Metal*, 1995, 26.

'Garbage'

Released as the fourth single from *Machiavelli*, 'Garbage' at times feels like something of a self-fulfilling prophecy for TISM. Lyrically, the song chiefly refers to the ongoing tendency of old trends reappearing in an almost cyclical fashion, speaking largely to the topic in relation to music.

Much of the song's meaning is summed up in the second verse alone: 'I know that we should separate our garbage, the environment will give us thanks. It's going too far when teenagers recycle their parents' adolescent angst.'

At the time of the song's release, musical culture was largely defined by the rise of the alternative scene, yet underscored by the ongoing 1960s revival. In their 1994 book *Generation Ecch*, Jason Cohen and Michael Krugman noted that those of the era 'excessively idealised the boomers' coming-of-age decade', sarcastically describing the 1960s as representative of 'a happier, better world: a giddy time of campus unrest, drug abuse, armed conflict in the streets and in the rice paddies'.[54]

Indeed, the music of the 1960s found itself making a comeback at the time in a way that would occasionally feel more trite and derivative in regards to new artists creating and old artists hitting the comeback circuits, and old and repetitive when it came to revisiting an era only a few decades old.[55]

---

[54] Jason Cohen and Michael Krugman, *Generation Ecch!: The Backlash Starts Here* (New York: Gallery Books, 1994), 161.
[55] This is most evident in the genres such as Madchester of the 1980s and Britpop of the 1990s, whereby influences of late 1960s pop and psychedelia combined to create a popular, though derivative, subgenre of rock.

Flaubert would reflect on the music of the 1990s in 2018, using the term 'the birth of retro' in relation to the period:

> The 1990s was the first era where there were a lot of bands coming through who listened to their parents' records because they were cool. Prior to that, the idea of emulating your parents' favourite bands would have been a horrible concept, but suddenly the parents of the 1970s and the 1980s were birthing children who were coming out and starting bands.[56]

As the English music journalist Simon Reynolds would later muse in his book *Retromania: Pop Culture's Addiction to Its Own Past*, 'Could it be that the greatest danger to the future of our music culture is . . . its past?'[57]

For TISM at the time, the question that surrounded this trend was simply 'why?'. In a verse that appeared only on the single version of 'Garbage', the band made their stance clear: 'What's so good about the '60s that we gotta keep rewindin' the clock? You know the best thing about the '60s? They'd never heard of "classic rock"'.

Regardless of the increasingly ubiquitous approach to mining the depths of decades gone by for inspiration, there was a sense of irony at play throughout most of the track. Namely in that the lyrical idea of recycling one's garbage had been itself recycled from an earlier song, with more recycling soon to take place.

---

[56] Cowell, *Take 5*.
[57] Simon Reynolds, *Retromania: Pop Culture's Addiction to Its Own Past* (London: Faber & Faber, 2011), ix.

In July 1991, the band recorded a demo titled 'Save the World', which would be an early version of 'If You're Ugly, Forget It', as released on *The Beasts of Suburban*. Touching on the notion of apparent disasters (musical or otherwise) making a comeback, the demo marks an early appearance of the 'Monday night is '50s night, Tuesday night is '60s night, Wednesday night is '70s night, Friday night is Thursday night' line that would later appear in 'Garbage'.

While much of the music (and the lyric relating to saving the world and recycling one's garbage) would be recycled for the studio version of 'If You're Ugly, Forget It', early demos of what would later become 'Garbage' show the band's swift transition to keyboard-heavy instrumentation, with de la Hot-Croix Bun's synthesizer lines serving as the backbone of the track.

The recycling concept reappeared on the single release of 'Garbage' in January 1996, with the single's artwork simply reading, 'This is garbage. Don't recycle it.' However, the contents itself were remixes of two TISM tracks. One was Maddy's remix of 'Strictly Loungeroom' from the 'Greg! The Stop Sign!!' single (retitled 'Strictly Refuse'), and the others were three remixes of 'Garbage' by Snog's Thrussell and Bourke, titled 'Garbage', 'Junk' and 'Rubbish'.

Following their work on the 'Jung Talent Time' single, Thrussell and Bourke had discussed the potential of remixing '(He'll Never Be An) Ol' Man River', though the rush-release of the single left the pair without adequate time to do so.

The remixed version of 'Garbage' was largely the same as the studio version, albeit with more dance beats and synth lines, the inclusion of an unused verse and a brief intro which opened many TISM concerts. The result was well-received by Flaubert, who felt it was an improvement on the album version.

'Rubbish' was much similar in its approach, removing the vocals and adding in a number of new musical elements to result in a dance-heavy number. 'Junk', however, was a stark contrast to the version that inspired it. Beginning with the introductory toasting from Jamaican reggae artist Mikey Dread's 1979 track 'Saturday Night Style', much of the track lifts from English dub artists Henry & Louis' 'Bobimore Dub' before leaning heavy on bass, drums and limited vocals to create a largely 'raggamuffin instrumental', which had been used as opening music for the *Machiavelli* tour.[58]

Fittingly, the remix of 'Junk' was *itself* recycled somewhat the following year when Thrussell and Bourke used much of the track (minus the Dread sample and sparse vocals) to inform 'Amphibious Premonitions Bureau', which appeared on their Soma project's *Stygian Vistas* EP.

Recalled Thrussell:

> We liked it, and not wanting to be uncivil about it, that music was entirely our creation. I remember Michael Lynch raising an eyebrow about it, but we felt entirely justified in saying, 'Well, we've created this music for TISM and that's all fine, but we'd like this one.'

In a slightly full-circle moment, Soma's *Stygian Vistas* was released in Australia on the Prozaac Recordings label – which was itself run by Lynch and Adam Yazxhi.

---

[58] TISM, *Junk Mail List*, December 8, 1995.

Could it be that all art is cyclical and that new ideas are simply standing on the metaphorical shoulders of giants as they are informed by what came before? Likely; though TISM's lyrical urging of 'Do you want to save the world? Don't recycle garbage' feels much more succinct.

'Lose Your Delusion II'

In TISM's discography, 'Lose Your Delusion II' stands apart as one of the rare tracks to have received another look-in. While numerous songs grew and evolved when taken to the live stage, only a stark few received a musical make-over in some capacity.[59] 'Lose Your Delusion II', however, seemed like a concerted effort to update the version TISM had first committed to tape only a few years earlier.

The first iteration of the song appeared on the *Australia the Lucky Cunt* EP in late 1993. While the EP's inner artwork had already parodied Guns N' Roses' logo, 'Lose Your Delusion' was in direct reference to the Los Angeles rock outfit's twin albums *Use Your Illusion I* and *II*, both released on the same day in September 1991.

Though not particularly resonant in terms of mainstream success (the EP would only peak at #131 on the national charts), it is heavily representative of TISM in 1993. Alongside its guitar-heavy composition (which it owes to the then-nascent inclusion of Blackman on guitar), it lyrically shows

---

[59]'Defecate on My Face' is arguably one of the most prominent examples, having been released as three different versions between 1986 and 1988 alone.

TISM satirically urging for the listener to 'choose beauty over truth' – to paraphrase the name-checked John Keats's 1819 poem 'Ode on a Grecian Urn' – and tune into the rising trend of 'infotainment' as opposed to respected news broadcasters on stations such as SBS.[60] Whereas Keats's line '"Beauty is truth, truth beauty," – that is all / Ye know on earth, and all ye need to know'[61] equated beauty with truth, TISM's lyric subverts the original meaning as they privilege beauty, thus underlining the devaluation of the concept of truth.

Perhaps an indication that the track was never intended to be re-recorded was in its name, which lacked the numerical suffix that Guns N' Roses' album featured. Indeed, 'Lose Your Delusion II' was never supposed to be revived, and the earlier rock-based version might well have survived quite well had *Machiavelli* not been made.

The newer version is, for all intents and purposes, an updated rendition of the track, complete with bubbling synth lines, thick bass and a larger chorus. Much of the new version was inspired by Psychick Warriors ov Gaia's 'Dizzy Drift Mix' of The Golden Palominos' 'Prison of Rhythm' – a track which Flaubert had discovered during his foray into the world of trance music. Largely influential in terms of style and feel, it provides an idea of the hypnotic approach TISM were aiming for on this version.

However, when directly compared, the initial version of 'Lose Your Delusion' feels outdated as it stands in the shadow

---

[60] This approach was clearly satirical given the titular subject of later song 'What Nationality Is Les Murray?' was also an SBS presenter at the time.
[61] John Keats, *The Poems of John Keats* (New York: Dodd, Mead & Company, 1905), 195.

of its successor. Though the atmospheric synth can still be heard in its intro, the rough guitar lines from Blackman feel like a fuzzy moment in time, while Hitler-Barassi's vocals are jarring when compared to his work on the later version.

Fittingly, 'Lose Your Delusion II' feels like the link between two worlds for TISM. While indicative of the method they were using to revitalize their sound, those who might have complained about the new approach still have a sonic life-preserver by way of an earlier favourite.

'!UOY Sevol Natas'

By the time the 1990s arrived, conservatives around the world had already fallen victim to the 'Satanic Panic', a moral panic in which fears of satanic ritual abuse had spread far and wide. Perpetuated in part due to the discredited 1980 book *Michelle Remembers* by the Canadian psychiatrist Lawrence Pazder and the McMartin preschool trial of the late 1980s, the satanic panic resulted in numerous theories as to its cause, with heavy metal music often being used as a scapegoat. Notable examples would include blaming Ozzy Osbourne for the 1985 suicide of John Daniel McCollum or Marilyn Manson for the 1999 Columbine High School massacre.[62]

The alleged role of heavy metal music in the satanic panic reached widespread prominence in 1990 when the English group Judas Priest were accused of causing a 1985 incident

---

[62] Maureen Mahoney, 'Is Litigation the "Suicide Solution"? Performers, Producers and Distributors' Liability for the Violent Acts of Music Listeners', *Touro Law Review* 16, no. 1 (1999): Article 6.

in the United States where twenty-year-old James Vance and eighteen-year-old Raymond Belknap shot themselves, the latter fatally. The group was accused of inserting subliminal messages into their music to inspire fans to harm themselves, though the resulting lawsuit was ultimately dismissed by a judge who labelled the alleged messages as purely 'coincidental'.[63]

Judas Priest frontman Rob Halford later claimed the idea of inserting subliminal messages was a bad business model, noting he'd rather insert phrases that urged fans to 'buy more of our records'.[64]

However, the notion of heavy metal bands placing subliminal messages into their records persisted, and by 1991, TISM had adopted the topic for their own music, working on a track titled 'Subliminal Satanic Message'. The group had recorded a demo version in July, with their song subverting the titular theme by making the central message as overt as possible.

That same month, another version titled 'Subliminal Satanic Message/Go the Knuckle', would expand upon the lyrics, and included a sample of the solo from Otis' 'Country Girl' that would later be included in 'All Homeboys Are Dickheads'. The theme of the track was abundantly clear from its opening lyric: 'Metallica are a bunch of wusses, there ain't no reason to hide behind no backward satanic message; just go off and suicide.'

---

[63] Timothy E. Moore, 'Scientific Consensus and Expert Testimony: Lessons from the Judas Priest Trial', *Skeptical Enquirer* 20, no. 6 (1996): 37.
[64] David Van Taylor, dir., *Dream Deceivers* (3-D Documentaries, 1992).

A polished version of 'Subliminal Satanic Message' would be recorded in July 1993 with Cohen during the *Australia the Lucky Cunt* sessions, though it wouldn't be released until its inclusion on the *Collected Recordings* box set.

Regardless, the song would later be revived during the sessions for *Machiavelli*, with one demo being a guitar-heavy version of the song, albeit with lyrics delivered using the melody that would later be utilized on 'Garbage'.

Inspiration would seemingly strike from the lyrics of 'Subliminal Satanic Message' ('Someone please play this song backwards, "Satan loves you" is what I said. God knows it's pretty boring forwards, and one more fan is dead'), with a new track titled '!UOY Sevol Natas' emerging during the *Machiavelli* sessions. An early version of the song would be largely guitar-led, in line with the band's sound from the 1993 era, before the inclusion of more electronic instruments on the final version.

Unlike 'Subliminal Satanic Message' (which was far from subliminal), '!UOY Sevol Natas' is far more subtle in its musical delivery and lyrical composition, with swirling synths and a blues-folk guitar solo from Blackman featuring prominently. It's a notable departure from TISM's usual 'firing on all cylinders' approach, this time allowing a moment of space and reflection within the song – something oddly paradoxical for a song focussing on elements of satanism.

'What Nationality Is Les Murray?'

For many Australians in the 1990s and 2000s, the name Les Murray was synonymous with soccer. Immigrating to Australia from Hungary at the age of eleven in 1957, Murray joined SBS in 1980, eventually becoming a football commentator and presenter of programmes such as *World Soccer* and *The World Game*.

Alongside being credited as helping popularize the sport within Australia, Murray's distinctive accent and linguistic versatility made him a prominent and capable broadcaster. For casual viewers though, his origins remained something of a mystery, and in the early 1980s, details about Murray were somewhat scarce. As TISM found themselves coalescing, Flaubert's still-unreleased solo work resulted in a number of early recordings, including one titled 'What Nationality Is Les Murray?'[65]

As the title suggests, the song is predominantly built around the mystique which surrounded Murray's ethnicity, while also highlighting his abilities to master the pronunciation of players' names during broadcasts. As with the studio version from 1995, the earliest-recorded version of the song also features samples from the same Italian soccer match which saw ACF Fiorentina beat Torino FC 4-1 at Stadio Artemio Franchi on 22 January 1984.

The earliest version was slower and featured elements of industrial instrumentation, while Flaubert's vocals were somewhat more eerie. As the track was revived for the *Machiavelli* album, it was given a more upbeat reimagining, adding in a catchier chorus, and a segment which lists forty-five countries, none of which were the correct answer; Hungary.

---

[65] Cowell, *Only the Shit You Love*, 10 November 2021.

The track does, however, end with the spoken phrase 'Éljen Magyarország', which translates to 'long live Hungary'.

The song's release also inspired a brief relationship between TISM and Murray. In 1994, the band had cited the broadcaster as their favourite poet (jokingly conflating him with the Australian poet of the same name), claiming, 'he's good because he also does the soccer on SBS'.[66] In 1995, Murray would take part in a scripted interview alongside the album's release, and in March 1996, he would make a slightly satirical appearance on triple j's J Files segment on TISM:

> When I first heard the song, I was delighted. Not because of my involvement with it, but because of the attention it would draw to the world game; the beautiful game [. . .] Personal advancement is of no consequence to me, it's the advancement of football that is most important to me.[67]

Murray and TISM's relationship notably culminated with the band's success at the 1995 ARIA Awards.[68] Nominated for Best Independent Release alongside Def FX, Ed Kuepper, Magic Dirt and Single Gun Theory, no members of the band attended the ceremony on 2 October,[69] instead recruiting Murray to accept the award should they win.

Upon their winning announcement, Murray took to the stage to deliver an acceptance speech, quieting the audience

---

[66] TISM, 'The TISM Guide to Literature', media release, 1994.
[67] Les Murray, *The J Files*, triple j, 28 March 1996.
[68] ARIA, *The ARIA Report* No. 295, Australian Recording Industry Association, 8 October 1995.
[69] Online sources claim the ARIA Awards occurred on 20 October, though the ARIA Report disputes this.

by claiming 'this is serious' as scattered cheers rang out, before switching to his prepared remarks:

> In the immortal words of the great Hungarian centre-forward Nandor Hidegkuti: *amikor eljön a forradalom, a zeneipar lesz az első, amely menni fog. Köszönöm szépen* – thank you very much.[70]

Given his celebratory cadence, the crowd erupted into cheers, despite not knowing what Murray had actually said. When TISM released their 1998 VHS compilation *Gold! Gold!! Gold!!!* (which prominently featured Murray), a clip of the incident was subtitled to read, 'The music industry is a septic boil on the buttocks of humanity. I hope you all die a horrible death'.[71]

However, when accurately translated, Murray's speech actually claims, 'When the revolution comes the music industry will be the first to go. Thank you very much.'

'Greg! The Stop Sign!!'

Given its status as one of the band's biggest hits, 'Greg! The Stop Sign!!' has the dubious honour of being salvaged from the potential fate of becoming an overlooked B-side. The reason for this near-brush with relative obscurity came down to TISM having felt embarrassed by a song they deemed to be somewhat too corny for their next major project.

---

[70] ARIA, 'TISM Wins Best Independent Release | 1995 ARIA Awards', YouTube, 4 September 2019. https://www.youtube.com/watch?v=9KAGNUdJvvI.
[71] *Gold! Gold!! Gold!!!*, VHS, edited by Guy Richards, Warner Music, 1998.

It's quite understandable, however. One of the most notable aspects of 'Greg! The Stop Sign!!' is the fact that its chorus is something of a style parody of The Beach Boys thanks to its heavy use of harmonizing. Utilizing Cheese's near scat-like vocals and heavy chorus harmonization like the Californian group's cover of The Regents' 1961 doo-wop single 'Barbara Ann',[72] much of the song is akin to something of a public service announcements for misguided youth.

The title of the song harkens back to a 1991 advertising campaign from Victoria's Transport Accident Commission which was officially called 'Country Kids'. In the commercial, a group of four youths are seen driving as two of the passengers begin to tussle with each other. The behaviour distracts the driver who misses a stop sign, causing the fourth passenger to call out 'Darren!' as their car is struck by an oncoming vehicle.[73]

By 1993, TISM had adopted the advertisement's messaging for one of their onstage diatribes, performing a piece titled 'Have You Ever Met . . .' for the crowd at their Pushover festival appearance on 20 November. Alongside themes that would later carry over to the final version of the song, much of the diatribe's penultimate verse would be repurposed for the track, with the title itself making its first appearance within:

The best looking boy in your secondary school
Will become a moustached accountant;

---

[72] The doo-wop aspects of both *Machiavelli*'s artwork and the sound of 'Greg! The Stop Sign!!' are coincidental, though hard to ignore.
[73] Transport Accident Commission Victoria, '"Darren" Country Kids TAC tv ad', YouTube, 2 December 2009. https://www.youtube.com/watch?v=zXiyFkJMAPI.

The biggest rebel who breaks every rule
Always becomes the public servant;
The brainiest kid who always gets A's
Will be a junkie before twenty-five;
That school captain who gets all the praise
Will scream, 'Greg, the stop sign!' just before she dies.[74]

By early 1994, the song had begun to take shape within the studio, with rehearsals presenting a slower version whose lyrics were largely similar to the final release. In lieu of The Beach Boys-esque chorus, simple shouted vocals were employed instead, before devolving into a refrain of their earlier track 'The Ballad of Paul Keating', repurposing the lyric 'Paul is dead' to instead appear as 'Greg is dead'.

As the track evolved across further rehearsals, the chorus line was altered to mimic The 5th Dimension's 'Aquarius/Let the Sunshine In',[75] while further lyrics were also added to the bridge, ultimately reappropriating two verses from 1992's then-unreleased 'Consumption Tax' for the bridge. The latter song had been demoed as early as October 1991, having adopted some melodies from an earlier demo titled 'Too Cool for School, Too Stupid for Life'.

By the middle of 1994, the track had adopted its now-famous harmonized vocals and introduced a guitar solo from Blackman, which would later be solidified as an almost note-perfect interpolation of The Shadows' 1961 instrumental, 'F.B.I.'

---

[74] TISM, 'TISM's Occasional Pieces'.
[75] Officially titled 'Medley: Aquarius/Let the Sunshine In (The Flesh Failures)' and released in 1969, this single was a medley of two songs originally written for the 1967 musical *Hair*.

Lyrically, the song's focus is summed up in a 1994 rehearsal which sees Hitler-Barassi pre-empting his performance by claiming it's 'a song about growing up'.[76] However, the superficial summation is expanded upon elsewhere, with a press release for the single describing its message as 'one of complete despair, hopelessness and nihilism delivered with a cheery "missing you already!" McDonald's employee-of-the-month grin'.[77]

Noting an 'apparent incongruous juxtaposition of surf harmonies and jungle trance beats' throughout, the press release also compares the track to Doris Day's 1956 hit 'Que Sera, Sera (Whatever Will Be, Will Be)' and underlines the nihilist aspect by claiming that 'no matter how surprisingly your future turns out, you'll probably die a horrific death in a semi-trailer accident anyway'.[78]

In a 1995 interview, Hitler-Barassi expanded upon the concept somewhat, describing 'an innate, primitive, rigorous, almost fascist conservatism' that lies within the heart of 'most violent, rebellious rock'n'roll loving of adolescents'.[79]

He adds:

Deep in the heart of everyone is a mediocre suburban person. That's what 'Greg! The Stop Sign!!' is about. When you grow up

---

[76] Some irony may be present in the fact a track whose message seems to provide advice for the teenage listener was preceded by a press release titled 'Why We Should Hate Teenagers: A Users Guide' in 1994.
[77] TISM, 'Greg! The Stop Sign!!', media release, July 1995.
[78] Ibid.
[79] Brett Buttfield, 'Will Success Spoil Hitler-Barassi?', *dB Magazine* 99, 16 August 1995.

you find out who you really are and in the end it's not very attractive.[80]

It was Williams who ultimately realized the potential of 'Greg! The Stop Sign!!', salvaging it from the heap of potential B-sides and championing it as the record's third single. Though the success of '(He'll Never Be An) Ol' Man River' had helped TISM hit the mainstream, it was the release of 'Greg! The Stop Sign!!' that gave the band the one-two blow to cement their staying power throughout 1995.

The single was officially released on 6 August, peaking at #59 on the ARIA singles chart under a month later. The sleeve of the single itself reworked the cover of the 1987 novel 'Out of Control' from the young adult series *Sweet Valley High*, with the artwork being repurposed so as to give a nod to its focus on themes relating to teenagers.

Its accompanying music video, largely filmed at the St Kilda Football (Australian Rules Football) Club's home ground, Moorabbin Oval, was noted for its tie-in to the 1995 campaign to save the team. In June, the club launched its 'Save Our Saints' campaign as a way to raise the $1.5 million needed to avoid a merger with another team.[81]

TISM's involvement with the campaign was explained by footballer Justin Peckett (who would appear in the music video for the song alongside Shane Wakelin, Josh Kitchen and Chris Hemley); he claimed 'at least one of the band members

---
[80] Ibid.
[81] Peter Carter, 'Saints Set $1.5m Goal to Stay Intact', *The Canberra Times*, 29 June 1995, 22.

was a mad Saints fan'.[82] In fact, the club had previously been the focus of TISM's 1992 song 'Father and Son', with Flaubert namechecking then-current players Nicky Winmar and Tony Lockett.

Directed by Mark Hartley (who would win an ARIA in 2000 for his work with Madison Avenue), the clip would see most of the band performing inside the clubrooms and on Moorabbin Oval, interspersed with clips of a party and black-and-white shots of fake films reviewed for SBS' *The Movie Show*.

Peckett recalled:

> The club asked a few players if they would be interested, and there weren't too many takers, but I put my hand up straight away. I was the only one at the club that really appreciated the band and their music. So, it was quite a thrill, but for everyone else, it was probably just a pain in the arse.[83]

'It's one of my proudest moments, which says a little bit about my career maybe', he would later admit.[84]

'I think what [St Kilda] were expecting was a Tina Turneresque[85] celebration of athleticism and manly endeavour,

---

[82] Ed Carmine, 'TISM! How a Balaclava-Clad Band Helped Save the Saints', *Zero Hanger*, 18 February 2022. https://www.zerohanger.com/tism-how-a-balaclava-clad-band-helped-save-the-saints-97849/.
[83] Ibid.
[84] Stupid Old Channel, 'Matt Meets St Kilda Legend JUSTIN "FRANKIE" PECKETT | Matt Your Heroes', YouTube, 18 February 2021. https://www.youtube.com/watch?v=4QNbTClEAAM.
[85] Tina Turner became synonymous with the National Rugby League in the 1980s and 1990s, with her song 'The Best' being deemed an unofficial anthem for the sport following its use in a highly-successful advertising campaign.

but what they got was a homoerotic abrogation of all that they stand for', Hitler-Barassi said shortly after the video's release.[86]

Flaubert would admit later in 2021 that he was absent for much of the filming (as was Cheese), though he did make a small cameo in the 'boot room' of the club:

> [It was] yet another in a long list of TISM film clips that I was mainly not in attendance at. This is the sort of band that you can, actually, not attend a film clip and get away with it.[87]

TISM's involvement with the club would extend beyond the video, and on 6 September, the band would also perform at The Palace in St Kilda as part of the SOS Benefit Concert, which would also feature artists like Cosmic Psychos and The Fauves and would ultimately aid in raising $40,865.[88]

A second clip for the song was also produced as part of the 1995 ARIA Awards ceremony, and featured the group dressed in their fat businessmen costumes, miming the song in an elevator alongside comedians and actors Michael Veitch, Tony Martin and Mick Molloy; singer Merril Bainbridge; and broadcaster, comedian and event host Richard Stubbs.

Filmed at the former Cadbury-Schweppes House on St Kilda Road, Martin remembers the filming as being chaotic, with the video designed to be a pre-recorded live performance in lieu of the band actually attending the ARIAs:

---

[86] Buttfield, 'Will Success'.
[87] Stupid Old Channel, 'Matt Meets Music Legend DAMIAN COWELL | Matt Your Heroes', YouTube, 4 March 2021. https://www.youtube.com/watch?v=aEzhWl4SqN8.
[88] Carmine, 'TISM!'.

We're going, 'Hang on, isn't there already a great video for this song?' And it was like, 'Yeah, this is just going to be on the ARIAs'. The premise was we're in a lift, but presumably it was the lift at the building where the ARIAs were on. All I remember is that we were there, they're jumping around, and we totally fucked that lift; it's amazing we didn't plummet to our deaths.

Like '(He'll Never Be An) Ol' Man River', the track would feature on triple j's annual Hottest 100 countdown in January 1996, reaching #10, one position lower than its preceding single.

'Play Mistral for Me'

Though the title of 'Play Mistral for Me' would later be described as a 'shithouse pun'[89] thanks to its loss of topicality, all aspects of the song are a great example of TISM's layered cultural references. The title itself is a reference to the 1971 Clint Eastwood film *Play Misty for Me*, which sees Eastwood's character stalked by an obsessive fan, while Mistral is an Australian home appliances brand, manufacturing items such as fans.

Its loss of topicality refers to the fact that when the lyric had first been penned in the early 1990s, Mistral had been the subject of two product recalls after their fans were deemed to pose a fire hazard.[90] By 1995, this controversy had somewhat

---

[89] Cowell, *Only the Shit You Love*, 13 October 2021.
[90] Senator Michael Tate, 'Mistral Gyro Aire Fans', media release, 25 November 1991.

faded from the public view, though the remainder of its lyrical content remained topical.

Originally titled 'I'm Head of the Mark Chapman Fan Club' in reference to the convicted murderer of John Lennon, the song largely makes references to notable figures whose fan bases were the source of major controversy. These include the likes of The Beatles' 'Helter Skelter' inspiring cult leader Charles Manson, the death of Meredith Hunter at The Rolling Stones' Altamont Free Concert, the stabbing of tennis player Monica Seles by a fan of Steffi Graf and the murder of the Colombian soccer player Andrés Escobar, amongst others.

The opening line of the chorus is lifted from Oscar Wilde's 1897 poem 'The Ballad of Reading Gaol', and first appeared in a demo titled 'Oscar Wilde Thing' from March 1991. The demo's lyrics also referred to fans' relationship with their idols and served as inspiration for a later guitar-heavy demo titled 'You're Only as Good as Your Fans' from the same era.

Another softer version of the song was also recorded around the same time under its original title. Like 'All Homeboys Are Dickheads', the track is also notable within the context of the record as being one of the only songs to feature live drums from Flaubert, while its lengthy ending is a rare moment of sparsity as Blackman and de la Hot-Croix Bun showcase their respective talents.

The track also includes a brief section which could be considered the band's closest brush with hip-hop by way of a verse from Hitler-Barassi, though it's more accurately a stylized parody of the genre given its explicit references to Public Enemy and serves as something of a callback to 'All Homeboys Are Dickheads'.

'How Do I Love Thee?'

Though largely unacknowledged within their wider discography, 'How Do I Love Thee?' marks another interesting example of how TISM's work was largely evolutionary, with portions of certain tracks being utilized in later compositions to form something wholly different. In this particular case, the roots of 'How Do I Love Thee?' can be traced back to some of the band's earliest work.

Between September and October 1983 – a matter of weeks after I Can Run played their last show and before TISM played their first – the group would record their fourth bedroom tape, *It's Novel! It's Unique! It's Shithouse!*. This tape included the tracks 'When You're Happy and You Know It, Kill Yourself' and 'Opium Is the Religion of the Masses', with the former being the song the group would use to open their performance at 3RRR's Battle of the Bands competition on 9 November 1985.

The success of this performance would see the group win time at Aztec Studios to record a handful of demos, with new recordings of 'When You're Happy and You Know It, Kill Yourself' and 'If You Want the Toilet, You're In It' going on to be named two of Melbourne community radio station 3PBS' top ten singles in May 1986.[91]

While 'When You're Happy and You Know It, Kill Yourself' would fade from setlists, its musical bed would instead be utilized for a newer version of 'Opium Is the Religion of the Masses', also known as 'Mein Kampf Fire Has Gone Out' due to the lyrics near its end. By 1990, the song was even floated for

---
[91] Anon, 'Top Ten Singles: 3PBS Selection', *The Age EG*, 16 May 1986, 6.

inclusion on *Hot Dogma*, with the track being demoed at Sing Sing Studios.

By 1995, the song had once again reared its head, with TISM utilizing the lyric 'Mein Kampf-fire is going out' for 'How Do I Love Thee?'. A strong example of TISM's energetic pop sensibilities, the track takes both its title and chorus from Elizabeth Barrett Browning's Sonnet 43 from 1845, while the lyrics appear to provide a cynical life cycle of how love can soon turn to disgust.

On the live stage, the track (where it was listed as 'Mein' on all setlists) didn't last long outside of the record's promotional cycle, and though enjoyable in the context of the record, it's best used as a way of seeing where TISM came from while showing where they were going.

'Jung Talent Time'

Though largely attributed to Andy Warhol, the famed quote 'in the future, everyone will be world-famous for 15 minutes' has hazy origins regarding its authorship since it first appeared in a programme for a 1968 Warhol exhibition in Stockholm.[92] Regardless of its original author, the quote's reference to fleeting fame has long been used in regard to those whose reasons for notability are questionable. At its core, 'Jung Talent Time' is a commentary on this fact, simply listing those who

---

[92] Olle Granath, 'With Andy Warhol 1968', Moderna Museet, Accessed 21 January 2024. https://www.modernamuseet.se/stockholm/en/exhibitions/andy-warhol-other-voices-other-rooms/with-andy-warhol-1968-text-ol/.

the band deem to have overstayed their brief flirtation with the spotlight.

With its title pairing the work of psychiatrist and psychoanalyst Carl Jung and long-running Australian variety programme *Young Talent Time*[93] to highlight the brevity of fame, the track is musically very simple, driven largely by Blackman's guitar work and Cheese's assertive bassline. Over the top, Hitler-Barassi recites a list of celebrities, before Flaubert uses the chorus to assert, 'Andy Warhol got it right, everybody gets the limelight; Andy Warhol got it wrong, 15 minutes is too long'.

Alongside names whose flame has since dimmed (including Jacko [former AFL footballer and media personality], Bros [English pop group] and Noeline Donaher [Australian reality television personality]), the list is a strong showing of names whose popularity had either peaked or were contemporary pop culture figures who were predicted to burn out soon. Some names, however, did increase in popularity or relevance over time (Pearl Jam, Rob Lowe and Camilla Parker Bowles, to name a few), while others seemed to have been included for the sake of humorous commentary on fame (including 'any performance artist', 'anyone called Trevor' and TISM themselves).

Hitler-Barassi later claimed the song was 'not just a list of easy targets, it's a list of failures', adding the themes of 'failure, of mediocrity, of not being able to live up to one's ideals, of not

---

[93] Hosted by singer Johnny Young, *Young Talent Time* ran from 1971 until 1988 on Channel 10, and featured young performers under the age of sixteen, with some – including Kylie Minogue and Tina Arena – launching successful careers as a result.

being able to live the life one wants' are deeply present within their work.[94]

He continued:

> I think it's part of the way we're approaching this fact that everything's a joke and we're a joke as well. And also we're not actually slagging these people off, we're swimming with them. Because when we say fifteen minutes is too long, that actually means some people had less than fifteen minutes in the whole scheme of things, but I'm not implying for a minute that Fairlie Arrow[95] shouldn't have done what she did.[96]

This song, however, has the notable honour of being the first song from the album released as a single, and thus, the first taste that the public had of TISM's new direction.

Following the album's recording, Lynch had spoken to Thrussell – whose Snog and Black Lung projects had performed better in markets such as Europe and the United States than in his native Australia – about whether he felt TISM had the potential to reach fans internationally:

> I didn't think the music would translate. The lyrics and the concepts are pretty Australian – and that's fine; that's not necessarily a disadvantage – but I didn't think it would work internationally. People wouldn't get the underlying humour.

---

[94] Sawford, 'You're Only As Jung', 17.
[95] Fairlie Arrow gained notoriety in December 1991 when the aspiring singer staged a fake abduction in pursuit of fame, with her disappearance generating widespread media attention at the time.
[96] Sawford, 'You're Only As Jung', 17.

I said, 'I would keep the lyrics and the concepts, and just do completely new music.'

Lynch commissioned Thrussell and then-Snog bandmate Bourke to craft a remix of the track, though the process actually involved the pair 'recreating the music completely' by deleting what TISM had recorded and mainly utilizing the vocals and guitar.

While Thrussell would later meet with Flaubert and Hitler-Barassi to discuss the track, receiving their approval of the remixes, keyboardist de la Hot-Croix Bun was less enthused. 'I remember getting a very agitated phone call from him, saying, "I've heard the remix – it's great, but there's a mistake; you've completely deleted all my keyboard parts"', he recalled. 'Being a slightly uppity little bastard, I said, "There's no mistake. We deleted them because they weren't any good."'

The result of Snog's input was a total of eight remixes which would be issued as a single, with the thirty-seven-minute release featuring no way of discerning between each. Future releases would see them identified by the addition of their track position, though this seemingly went against the very idea of satirizing the homogeneity present within the electronic scene of the era. Thrussell recalls:

> I think part of it was us taking the piss out of this remix culture as well. We sincerely liked this kind of music, but we also realized that there was a bombastic parody element involved in having eight remixes as well. There was a somewhat snide and darkly humorous kind of self importance in having so many remixes.

Given the music had been almost entirely recreated by Thrussell and Bourke, there's some slight irony in the fact the first single from TISM's new album had actually been largely made by Snog. However, no direct mention to Snog was made on the single release, something Thrussell assumes was likely a calculated move by Lynch. Thrussell notes:

> He's a pretty smart, savvy kind of guy, and he would've realized that TISM had a certain identity. I'm totally putting words into his mouth, but maybe he wanted to push that identity in certain directions, but also keep it subtle in other ways.

Given that TISM would effectively parody the new genre which they had entered by having a contemporaneous artist recreate their own music, and then mock the very remix culture they were promoting as they kicked off their album campaign, perhaps it was fitting that TISM themselves put their own name in the lyrics as an example of artists who'd overstayed their welcome?

'Aussiemandias'

Though contemporary critics may have heaped criticism on TISM for the content of '(He'll Never Be An) Ol' Man River', much retrospective condemnation towards the content of *Machiavelli* is largely centred around 'Aussiemandias'. The focus is due to the chorus lyric, which is directly lifted from Sly and the Family Stone's 1969 anti-discrimination song 'Don't Call Me Nigger, Whitey', and the other slurs included throughout.

In the context of the larger song, 'Aussiemandias' evokes the same message of racial harmony that Sly and the Family Stone's track appeals for, effectively pointing out the one unifying factor throughout humanity is a sense of widespread xenophobia. At the same time, however, it posits a 'do unto others' approach in its denunciation of racism.

The title may in fact refer to this mutual xenophobia and the lessened impact that the slurs therefore entail. A localized reference to Percy Bysshe Shelley's 1818 sonnet, 'Ozymandias', the source material refers to the ephemeral legacy of the titular ruler, and the inevitable decline of those in power. It could be argued that 'Aussiemandias' is therefore a reference to the fleeting impact that slurs have when put up against each other in a mutually exclusive manner. It's much more likely, however, to be in reference to their shared notions of cultural relativism and ethnocentrism.[97]

Regardless, the lyrics of 'Aussiemandias' turn it into something of a lightning rod for criticism and accusations of racism. Typically, the general construction of TISM's lyrics indicates there is more at play than what is on the surface. This was something addressed by Hitler-Barassi during a 2004 interview:

> What I feel is most effective and valuable about what we do is when we say stuff that everyone else is thinking and no one is saying. The whole idea of an artifice, as this band is, allows one

---

[97] Steve Bell, '20 Years Ago: How TISM's Third Album Helped Them Break Through, Despite Their Best Efforts', *The Music*, 1 May 2015. https://themusic.com.au/features/20-years-ago-tism-machiavelli-and-the-four-seasons-steve-bell/_fPuERATEhU/01-05-15.

to go too far, to make jokes about cancer – the sort of jokes that everyone makes to their mates down the pub.[98]

However, he noted a need to 'draw your own line' when it comes to lyrics that promote hate. 'TISM would never make a joke that supports a racist point of view, because racists can go get fucked', he added.[99]

The song's origins trace back to March 1991, when two versions of 'Aussiemandias' would be recorded with both Flaubert and Hitler-Barassi alternating lead vocal duties between the two. A later, more ferocious version was made in October and opens with a sample of 'Summer Nights' from *Grease*, which later appeared before live performances of the song. In this version, Hitler-Barassi handles the lead vocals while Flaubert takes the chorus.

In late 1992, a separate demo titled 'Tu E La Tua Razza Fa'un Culo', which loosely translates from Italian to 'You And Your Race Get Fucked', was recorded, with the titular lyrics having also appeared on the October 1991 version.

The coda of 'Aussiemandias' also attempts to seemingly underline the message of racial harmony suggested by the song, with the thirty-five-second piece asserting itself as a global sound collage of sorts. Comprising a drum beat and four vocal samples, the samples originated on records from various world music labels, including Tangent Records' 1976 release *Music in the World of Islam, 1: The Human Voice*, and Ocora's 1968 compilation, *Musique du Burundi*.

---

[98] Dwyer, 'The Phantom Menace'.
[99] Ibid.

For TISM, these samples were included on the 1992 Polestar Magnetics sample CD collection *XL1*, which the band had purchased during their trip to London in 1993. Further underlining the cultural interplay the inclusion of these samples seems to aim for, another Polestar Magnetics collection features some of these vocals on a track simply titled 'Ethno Vox'. Most likely, however, the inclusion of multicultural vocals was in reference to the growing trend of such practices, as seen through the likes of contemporary names such as Deep Forest.[100]

'Give up for Australia'

Following the September 1993 announcement that Sydney would host the 2000 Olympic Games, Australia once again found itself resting heavily on its not insignificant laurels in the world of sport. Instead of focusing on its larger achievements, the sports-mad atmosphere left much of the nationalistic focus reliant on the country's athletic prowess. It's this disparity, this pursuit of sporting greatness in lieu of more important achievements, that underpins much of 'Give up for Australia'.

Opening with Norman May's commentary of Australia's winning effort in the Men's 4 × 100-metre medley relay from the 1980 Moscow Olympics, the sample-heavy 'Give up for Australia' almost posits itself as something of a new anthem

---

[100] The aforementioned *Musique du Burundi* compilation was sampled by Michel Bernholc as Burundi Steiphenson Black for his 1971 single 'Burundi Black', which in turn informed the sounds of new wave groups such as Bow Wow Wow and Adam and the Ants.

for the country as it points towards Australia's apparent obsession with second-best. As ABC (Australian Broadcasting Corporation) broadcaster Phillip Adams said in a 2000 episode of *Late Night Live*, 'Australia rhymes with failure, and our great cultural statements are all about failure.'[101]

'May all our young Aussie swimmers be resigned to failure, may our nation state be always second rate', Hitler-Barassi intensely screams as May's distorted commentary, a relentless electronic beat, and pulsing synth work in unison.

Along with references to Australia's inability to create luminaries such as Norman Mailer and instead being content with the likes of May himself and the doomed Gallipoli landing of 1915, the track is complemented by a handful of samples, most prominently 'Sonny's Burning' from The Birthday Party. Two other samples – from Rolf Harris' 'I've Lost My Mummy' and his cover of John Williamson's 'Old Man Emu' – are also present.

'Give up for Australia' had been in the works since at least March 1991, with early recordings showing the lyrics arrived almost fully formed, though style was the main point of contention. Following a harder-rock version led by Hitler-Barassi, a bouncier rendition saw Flaubert take lead vocals, before a sweeping country-influenced version which seemed reminiscent of John Williamson emerged in May 1992. A later version from mid- to late 1993, the harsher 'Give Up', was later released on iTunes in 2009 and is ostensibly the final demo recorded before the studio version, and sees the group's experimentation with sounds coming to an end.

---

[101] Phillip Adams, *Late Night Live* (Radio National, 9 September 2000).

Fittingly though, the track also seems to be an encapsulation of TISM's own self-deprecating attitude that pervades much of their work. While they themselves have expressed this sort of attitude in both interviews, music and lyrics,[102] 'Give up for Australia' almost contextualizes it by way of addressing the wider problem and how it's embraced by the country as a whole. Live performances would feature a stuffed kangaroo – one of Australia's most prominent national symbols – held aloft before the audience in an almost jingoistic portrayal of national pride, while other members would mock-shoot it.

During the preparation for their 1998 album, *www.tism.wanker.com*, TISM touched upon similar themes on the unreleased 'Choose Lose', whose lyrics would later be reappropriated in the live favourite, 'Sickie': 'Stop winning, get beat; come second, admit defeat; don't bother, have a rest; let the others be the best'. Notably, 'Choose Lose' also bears musical and lyrical similarities with 'Celebrate the Failure', a 2000 song from The Fauves who would support TISM at live shows in 1998.

'Philip Glass's Arse'

In stark contrast to the rest of *Machiavelli*, 'Philip Glass's Arse' is a jarring stylistic left-turn for TISM, albeit one relegated to the end of the album as a hidden track.

---

[102] As 'We Are the Champignons' from 1990's *Hot Dogma* states; 'We'll be the first in the neighbourhood to say without a doubt, "we're no good"'.

Officially untitled on the record, the only acknowledgement of its existence comes from the lyrics' inclusion at the end of 'Give up for Australia' in the liner notes. However, the song had been mentioned in late 1993, when it was included in a press release offering alternate lyrics for songs on *Hot Dogma*, suggesting them as a replacement for 'It's Novel; It's Unique; It's Shithouse', and to be performed in the style of Stephen Cummings (solo artist and former frontman of Melbourne rock band The Sports). They said:

> The Top 40 is full of pop songs – so are G.W. McLennan [frontman of Brisbane rock group The Go-Betweens] albums. So how come he's got the intellectual standing of Aristotle? Either he writes verse/chorus or I've got my head up Philip Glass's arse. ('Philip Glass's arse' – rather hard to say, that. Sorta catchy, though.)[103]

By the time TISM made reference to Glass, the American composer and pianist had enjoyed a career for over thirty years. Famed for his work in the world of minimalism, his name was often associated with the pretence that accompanies far more 'arty' styles of music. Thus, such a title seemed appropriate for such a vastly different song from TISM.

The track was one of the rare times in which Blackman showcased his musical dexterity largely alone. A career musician prior to joining TISM in the early 1990s, Blackman had studied under various accomplished composers, and upon completing a degree at Melbourne State College, he applied

---

[103] TISM, 'Hot Dogma: Re-issued And Reconsidered'.

for a grant from The Australia Council to study overseas. Studying at Amsterdam's Sweelinck Conservatorium through 1984, he crafted a catalogue of commissioned compositions of various styles and genres as a result of his studies.[104]

The lyric for 'Philip Glass's Arse' was penned by Hitler-Barassi and describes a brief tryst between two individuals, punctuated with their coffee preferences. Given the previous reference to McLennan and the verbose lyrical similarities, it could be suggested the song was written in a manner reminiscent of The Go-Betweens.

Having not found a life anywhere else, Blackman suggested reimagining the song as a seventeenth-century madrigal (an Italian Renaissance style which flourished around the same time as Niccolò Machiavelli – the album's namesake) utilizing Melbourne vocalists Christine Storey on soprano vocals, Belinda Gillam on alto, Ewan Harwood on tenor and Bruce Raggatt on bass. The piece ultimately found its home on the record as a hidden track, preceded by one minute of silence.

Somewhat notably, TISM's appearances in the top ten of triple j's Hottest 100 countdown for 1995 had seen them place back-to-back with '(He'll Never Be An) Ol' Man River' and 'Greg! The Stop Sign!!' at #9 and #10, respectively. One year later, the 1996 countdown would see 'Ballad of the Skeletons' by the American poet Allen Ginsberg (and featuring Paul McCartney, Lenny Kaye and Glass) reach the #8 position – one placing higher than TISM.

---

[104] James Paull, 'Biography', James Paull, 24 April 2008. http://jamespaull.blogspot.com/2008/04/biography.html.

'The Last Soviet Star'

Commonly known as 'Russia' to fans due to a lack of official clarification, 'The Last Soviet Star' – as its official lyric sheet notes – was never a song that actually appeared on *Machiavelli* in a contemporary, commercial manner.

When it was first recorded at Platinum Studios with Maddy in December 1992, it was listed on the accompanying tape as 'Russia'. Though deemed as the 'official' title by some fans, this would therefore mean that other songs from this session – including 'Consumption Tax' and 'The Ballad of Paul Keating' – are therefore known by their own shorthand titles of 'Tax' and 'Keating', respectively.

By January 1993, the band had incorporated the song into their live sets, with a triple j broadcast of their performance at the Melbourne Big Day Out seeing the song both back-announced and listed on their setlists as 'Russia'. Again, this was likely due to the nature of shorthand adorning setlists for ease of communication.

In May 1995, a report in Adelaide's *dB Magazine* alerted readers to the fact that pre-release copies of *Machiavelli* would become 'an instant collector's item' due to the presence of 'the song "Russia" which has been pulled from the album and will never see the light of day, due to legal advice'. The article claimed the reasoning was because of the fact it 'borrowed heavily' from The Beatles' 1968 track 'Back in the U.S.S.R.', and had 'run into major legal problems with Paul McCartney and John Lennon's publishers'.[105]

---

[105] Anon, 'TISM VS The Beatles', *dB Magazine*, 10 May 1995.

Indeed, while the verses of the song largely consist of Hitler-Barassi namechecking a number of locations throughout Russia and surrounding regions, the chorus lifted from the bridge and final verse of The Beatles' earlier song.[106]

However, the legal issues weren't quite as reported. Instead of the song running afoul of publishers and being a near-repeat of 1993's Ken Done incident, its removal was purely due to caution and self-preservation. Performing some due diligence, Lynch had sent the track off to attain the proper permissions for use of the lyrics, but never received a reply.

Though simply releasing it without permission was a possible yet risky alternative, any objection would have resulted in pulling stock off the shelves once again. Instead of being fearful of litigation, the band's decision to leave the track off the album was mainly done so as to avoid any costs associated with another recall.

Williams remembers:

> I still think that was probably the best decision to make at the time. Maybe no one would have heard it, tacked on to the end of an album, but maybe it would have created problems. The prudent thing at the time was to leave the track alone.

The newly orphaned song did find its way online, however, where it was dubbed 'Russia' in accordance with contemporary reports, before a re-release of sorts occurred years later. When TISM made their debut onto iTunes in 2009, 'The Last Soviet

---

[106] Notably, 'Back in the U.S.S.R.' has been viewed as a parody of both The Beach Boys – akin to 'Greg! The Stop Sign!!' – and Chuck Berry, who is mentioned in 'Garbage'.

Star' had been appended to *Machiavelli* as a bonus track under its original title, though Flaubert had altered the 'offending' chorus lyric.

In 2023, a CD reissue of *Machiavelli* finally saw 'The Last Soviet Star' receive an official release when it was silently added to the end of the record, reclaiming its status as an unlisted hidden track.

4 The last Australian guitar hero

I wrote a song the other day, the best thing I ever sung. Another band began to play, there's always a better one. – 'Consumption Tax' (1992)

As is the case with most albums, the entirety of the recorded output which has sprung from the recording sessions rarely makes its way onto the final record in full. Often, many of these tracks are resigned to be released as B-sides, or sometimes kept back, never to be released at all. For TISM, these sessions resulted in a small handful of B-sides, a few demos which were never fully finalized, and a selection of spoken-word diatribes that were either recorded in-studio or simply performed live. This brief section aims to take a look at each of these songs, outlining the known facts as they relate to them.

B-Sides

Arguably the best-known 'offcuts' (for lack of a better term) are the B-sides released on the album's accompanying singles. The one likely most heard by casual fans would be 'Abscess Makes the Heart Grow Fonder', which appeared following the title track on the '(He'll Never Be An) Ol' Man River' single.

Featuring heavy guitars in verses and atmospheric synths in its bridge, the almost Shakespearean lyrics result in what TISM themselves labelled 'a charming little ditty about marriage'.[1]

An early version of the track was recorded under the name 'It's All Over' with working titles appearing to be 'We Deliver' and 'Does Fame Bring Forth' (though it doesn't bear any resemblance to the later diatribe 'Does Fame Bring Forth Madness?'). In 2009, an early demo of the song was released under the title 'The Note Stuck with a Magnet to Kurt Cobain's Fridge', which featured snippets of AC/DC's 1976 song 'Jailbreak' and Australian Crawl's 1983 song 'Reckless'.

The other song on the single, 'Dicktatorship', is a drastic departure from the rest of the tracks recorded in the album sessions. An entirely solo venture from Blackman, he complements his bluesy guitar talents against a rapid-fire stream of lyrics which ruminate on the unfulfilled sexual desires that inspire political careers.

An earlier version of the song was demoed and was starkly different in its composition. Instead of the solo effort it was released as, the demo featured Blackman's guitar joined by a drum machine and keyboard, while Hitler-Barassi delivered the lyrics at a rapid-fire pace. Though the lyrics are almost identical to the commercially released version, the delivery in the demo almost borders on hip-hop, prompting questions as to what happened in the studio to facilitate such a drastic change.

The following single, 'Greg! The Stop Sign!!', saw its title track followed by 'Strictly Loungeroom'. Somewhat dated in its references by modern standards, the song takes its title from

---

[1] TISM, 'I'm on the Drug That Killed River Phoenix'.

Baz Luhrmann's 1992 film *Strictly Ballroom*, and equates both its title and then-cutting-edge behaviour with the highly 'uncool' nature of the short-lived dancing competition programme *That's Dancin'*! Again pairing the traditional rock elements with TISM's newer electronic style, 'Strictly Loungeroom' features another example of Blackman's accomplished guitar playing by way of his powerful chorus riff and understated verse playing.

Like 'Greg! The Stop Sign!!', 'Strictly Loungeroom' also borrows a musical melody from the earlier 'Consumption Tax' and was later reimagined by Thrussell and Bourke as 'Strictly Refuse' for the 'Garbage' single release. Notably, this single version also includes lyrics by Hitler-Barassi not heard on the album version. One line, 'score me some despondency', is also featured on the inner artwork to the *Machiavelli* album, despite not appearing on the record itself.

The album's second single is rounded out by 'There's More Men in Children than Wisdom Knows', a title which had previously been adopted by TISM for a 1986 cassette recording and later featured on the label artwork for the black vinyl release of their '40 Years – Then Death' single the following year.

Paired with occasional effects designed to present Hitler-Barassi as performing the track live, the spoken-word diatribe recounts an incident at a venue in which Hitler-Barassi is accosted by drug takers who are revealed to be his family. Revealed to be a dream, the ironic recollection concludes with Hitler-Barassi noting the downsides to a world in which 'parents and teachers and policemen uniformed' acted like youths.[2]

---

[2] A similar narrative is explored on 1998's 'Opposite Day'.

Previously performed live at The Palace in St Kilda in January 1994 as a diatribe titled 'It Was at That Very Bar . . .',[3] the recording was somewhat notable for its appearance in the second TISM comic book, released that same month, with the first half of the issue featuring an illustrated retelling of the diatribe. While the diatribe features a number of references to celebrities (including Evan Dando, Kylie Minogue, Michael Jackson, Jennifer Keyte and Johnny Diesel), the commercially released version sees their surnames censored.

According to comic artist Mark Sexton, the version he had been provided ahead of his work on the second comic featured no censorship, and the decision to ultimately censor the comic in the same way the track itself would be was nothing more than a coincidence.

Diatribes

When the Gold accreditation of *Machiavelli* necessitated a re-release in 1996 with a bonus disc titled *Gold! Gold! Gold for Australia!*, the compilation of B-sides and remixes was complemented with five bonus tracks. The additional tracks were spoken-word diatribes from Hitler-Barassi and amounted to under five minutes of new material in total. 'I personally wouldn't spend the money myself, but I get the CD for free 'cause I'm in the band', Hitler-Barassi said.[4]

---

[3] TISM, 'TISM's Occasional Pieces'.
[4] Buttfield, 'The Hitler Diaries'.

One of these, '"Don't Believe the Hype" Is Hype', had previously been performed live as part of the band's 1992 *Beasts of Suburban* tour. Two others, 'Fuck 'Em, Fuck 'Em – The Lot of 'Em' and 'Does Fame Bring Forth Madness?', are abandoned after Hitler-Barassi stumbles in his recitation, though their full lyrics were later released online.

In all cases, these diatribes – which also include 'If You Ever Hear His Name, Harden Not Your Arteries' and 'Bash This up Your Ginger' – can be described as considered cultural critiques that reference pop culture, celebrity and art, though their swift run times and barebones recording styles may almost be designed to mock the need to include exclusive unheard material for bonus discs such as this.

Live Songs and Demos

Though the aforementioned tracks were officially released at the time, a number of other songs never quite made the leap into the band's contemporary recorded discography. In some cases, these were live tracks, such as the band's cover of New Waver's 'We're Gonna Get You after School', which was performed at their Big Day Out warm-up performance in Ocean Grove, Victoria on 11 January 1996, or 'Ate Breakfast off a Hooker's Tits', a diatribe evocative of 1988's 'And the Ass Said to the Angel: Wanna Play Kick to Kick?' (in reference to Nick Cave's then-forthcoming 1989 novel, *And the Ass Saw the Angel*) that was performed live during the *Machiavelli* album tour. Another, titled 'Protest Song', was performed once only on 27 April 1995, as part of the band's appearance on community television programme *Under Melbourne Tonight*.

Others still were those which never made it out of the writing sessions. Almost immediately after the sessions for 1993's *Australia the Lucky Cunt*, the band began penning more material, including 'Mighty River' – a guitar-heavy critique of those within the media spotlight, whose title bears no connection to the album's most prominent single, though the content itself appears somewhat related. Though a demo was recorded around mid-1993, the chorus of 'Mighty River' was later utilized in a diatribe titled 'Jesus Christ Might Love Me . . .', performed at the Collingwood Town Hall in October of the same year.[5]

By the first half of 1994, many more songs had begun to emerge through the band's writing sessions. While some of these were simply spontaneous musical ideas which didn't go anywhere, some appeared to influence other tracks on the eventual record.

'Stop the World' appears to have taken some cues from the already-recorded version of 'Aussiemandias'; 'Thesaurus Brontesaurus' feels reminiscent of the band's 1986 track 'I'm into Led Zep', though Hitler-Barassi's lyrical delivery is similar to what would appear on 'Play Mistral for Me', and the cadence of 'There's Only One Thing Worse' ostensibly informed the vocals of '!UOY Sevol Natas'.

Notably, the idea for 'Out, Out Damned Thirty-Second Spot' (in reference to a line from William Shakespeare's 1623 play *Macbeth*) was evidently shelved during these sessions, only to

---

[5] TISM, 'TISM's Occasional Pieces'.

be revived a decade later as 'Ken Bruce Has Gone Mad' on *The White Albun*.

Other songs still seemed to have not been pursued outside of the writing room, including tracks named 'Cancer', 'Right Turn Arrow', the bluesy 'Sammy' and 'Oh Great Gavan', a brief invocation in the name of the band's former manager.

5 The art-income dialectic

*You can break all the rules, but you're obsolescent
if you don't appeal to some shitface adolescent. –*
'Demographic Violence' (2004)

In the immediate aftermath of *Machiavelli*'s release, TISM weren't exactly an overnight commercial success. Given the performance of their previous records, this could very well have been an expected reality for the group. Slowly but surely, however, the record found its way into the top ten, won itself an ARIA Award, resulted in a UK tour and saw TISM inexplicably become minor celebrities of the Australian music scene in the process.

On 15 May, eleven days after its release, *Machiavelli* was designated triple j's Feature Album for the week, and on 20 May, TISM were the hosts of the long-running ABC television music programme *Rage*.

Unlike traditional hosts of the show who would simply introduce their favourite songs and clips, the pre-recorded appearance alienated its traditional viewership with their eclectic playlist. Alongside four consecutive Ted Mulry Gang songs, and clips from bands such as The Wiggles, Michael Bolton and Milli Vanilli, it featured theme songs from ABC current affairs programmes, and a fifteen-minute electronic press kit for Brian Eno.

The same night as TISM's *Rage* appearance, Flaubert entered Platinum Studios to mix a cover of AC/DC's 'For Those About to Rock' they had recorded that same month. The cover was intended to feature on an AC/DC tribute album that year, but due to the release of the similarly themed *Fuse Box* record only weeks later, the project was scrapped, and the single would not be released until 2020.

The following day, the new record debuted at #54 on the national ARIA Albums Chart and at #1 on the Alternative Albums Chart. Just three weeks later, *Machiavelli* would rise to its peak of #8 in the national charts before dropping to #9 the following week and slowly falling until its eventual exit in mid-September.

Though its chart peak would take more than a month to arrive, critical reception was largely positive upon *Machiavelli*'s release, too, save for a two-and-a-half star review from *Rolling Stone* which labelled the record as 'bland, throwaway boogie' and claimed it offered 'a passable amount of wit and a container-load of obviousness'.[1] The review continued: 'Doowop/rap parody is one thing, but there's unfortunate irony in the fact that much of *Machiavelli* is grievously slick and funky to a point beyond satire. Musical highlights are fleeting [. . .] Sometimes the great cultural terrorists appear to lack the courage of their convictions. Either that or their producer is

---

[1] Mark Demetrius, 'Machiavelli and the Four Seasons', *Rolling Stone Australia* 510, June 1995, 86.

incompetent.'[2] To their credit, *Rolling Stone* would give TISM a feature in their August issue, which was used to satirize the magazine, the review and the industry.[3]

In late May, the band continued their foray into various mediums when the first official TISM comic book was released via the AAARGH! Comics imprint, with Mark Sexton and John Petropoulos at the helm.

The idea for a comic had initially been floated as a replacement for a traditional press release for the record, following on from the comic created by Dillon Naylor for fellow Shock outfit The Fireballs. The initial brief was for a two-to-four-page press kit on the history of the group, which quickly expanded to twenty-one pages, harnessing the narrative of a young man taken on a Dickensian journey in which the members of TISM explain their origin story.

Sexton and Petropoulos met with Flaubert and Hitler-Barassi to discuss TISM's history at their Prahran rehearsal space, before Sexton took on the task largely solo, creating it in two and a half weeks between his usual duties with the *Bug & Stump* series. Typically, a similarly sized issue of *Bug & Stump* would take them two to three months to complete.

Sexton recalled:

> I spent about a day-and-a-half coming up with the entire comic. Part of its length was because it was an opportunity to do something cool, something that's a little bit different, and a challenge to try and do something that people would

---
[2] Ibid.
[3] TISM, 'Top Ten TISM: A Tragicomedy in One Act', *Rolling Stone Australia* 512, August 1995, 25.

find joy in reading. The joke being that in 1995, comics equaled lowbrow. That's what comics were at the time; no one respected them.

Upon submission to TISM's management, Sexton and Petropoulos suggested releasing it as a commercial product, with little more than a handshake agreement preceding its release.

Sales of the comic reached 5,500, necessitating a second printing and the permission to continue the series with a second volume. This time, Flaubert and Hitler-Barassi wanted to write it, with an initial idea comprising twenty-four pages of the same image nine times, only for the final page to feature a member telling the reader to 'fuck off'. Sexton defused the idea by telling Hitler-Barassi the concept was likely 'too arty'.

This second comic, issued in January 1996, comprised two illustrated Hitler-Barassi diatribes – 'There's More Men in Children than Wisdom Knows' and 'And the Ass Said to the Angel: Wanna Play Kick to Kick?' – alongside interstitial segments showing the effects of drug use, which somewhat salvaged Hitler-Barassi's earlier concept.

Given the nature of the material in the volume, Sexton and Petropoulos affixed a content warning to the cover and sent the comic to a legal representative at distributors Gordon & Gotch for their approval, ultimately receiving word that 10,000 copies would be printed. Twenty-four hours after its release, a recall for the comic was put into motion, with a single panel (featuring a TISM member saying, 'Take drugs kids . . . did me no harm') being deemed offensive enough to potentially warrant a ban.

The distributors recalled the product, though 2,500 copies had been sold in the two-week period in which it was available for sale. Prior to its recall, a third issue was planned, utilizing a story originally pitched for the second issue which focused on an embittered eighth member of TISM. By Sexton's own admission, it was 'probably just a fucking awful idea'.

* * *

By July 1995, TISM found themselves interviewed on the subscription television network Galaxy's Red channel (the precursor to Channel [V]) by Toni Pearen.[4] Prior to her work as a television presenter, Pearen had embarked on a successful musical career following a three-year run on the Channel 10 soap opera *E Street* from 1989 to 1992. Only eighteen months earlier, the thought of TISM being interviewed by one of Australia's most prominent television personalities would have seemed absurd. Further national exposure arrived in August when Tim Webster, host of Channel 10's *Sports Tonight*, aired the video for 'Greg! The Stop Sign!!' on the programme.[5]

In early October, TISM's nomination for Best Independent Release for *Machiavelli* at the ARIA Awards would see them take home their second trophy for the category, and in December, the band would release their *Collected Recordings* box set, which compiled the majority of their discography to that point, alongside a number of bonus tracks. Both the ARIA Award and the box set effectively closed out the band's most successful year to date.

---
[4] *Gold! Gold!! Gold!!!*.
[5] Ibid.

This mainstream success was arguably due to a mixture of factors, including both the controversy garnered by the release of their lead single and a structural shift at commercial radio network Triple M.

In mid-1995, Austereo appointed former triple j general manager Barry Chapman as the CEO of the Triple M network in an effort to increase the station's listener share.[6]

Chapman's plan to achieve this goal was relatively simple and largely involved switching the 'classic rock' format to a more contemporary sound. Resultantly, Triple M adopted a playlist which overlapped with triple j's by 'only 15%', yet used this more youth-oriented portion to help bring in more listeners from the eighteen to thirty-nine demographic.[7]

Initially, triple j had begun life in Sydney in 1975 on the AM dial under the 2JJ – or Double J – call sign. The station, a part of the ABC's radio network, experienced widespread popularity thanks to its non-commercial playlist and roster of hosts, and by August 1980, it had begun broadcasting on the FM band as 2JJJ, or triple j.[8] The station began a national expansion in October 1989, and by the middle of the 1990s, it had become a vital source of music for the country's growing alternative scene.[9]

'We've been accused of being more commercial [since the national launch], but our music tastes have changed very little

---

[6] Katherine Tulich, 'Triple J Leads A Radio Revolution', *Billboard*, 30 September 1995, 63.
[7] Neil Shoebridge, 'Radio Man Chases Ratings in a Race against Time', *Australian Financial Review*, 26 February 1996.
[8] Anon, '1975-1985: 40 Years of triple j', *The J Files*, Double J, 5 February 2015.
[9] Anon, '1985-1995: 40 Years of triple j', *The J Files*, Double J, 12 February 2015.

over the years', triple j's then-acting general manager Stuart Matchett said in late 1995. 'It's more a case of commercial radio now playing bands we've been playing all along. They've moved closer to us rather than the other way around.'[10]

The decision undoubtedly served TISM well. Though largely supported by community radio in their early days, the gradual spread to triple j helped to strengthen and expand their fanbase on a national level. The fact that triple j's airing of '(He'll Never Be An) Ol' Man River' was seen as the impetus for the single's rush-release was one thing, but for TISM to gain commercial airplay as Triple M attempted to mimic the government broadcaster's sound was another.

'While a TISM album previously would have sold 6,000 to 10,000 copies, its latest disc is well on the way to Gold (35,000 units)', Williams said in September 1995. 'That's the difference triple j can make.'[11]

TISM, however, asserted that their alternative radio success was due to the inclusion of 'naughty' words. 'Never mind that the song had very little to do with River Phoenix', they said. 'It was *naughty*. It had the word "drug" in it. Put down your glasses, ladies and gentlemen. Instant airplay.'[12]

By October, the album had sold 30,000 copies;[13] it received Gold accreditation on 23 January 1996; and by August, sales had reached 43,000 copies.[14] In 2024, Williams noted the

---

[10] Tulich, 'Triple J', 64.
[11] Ibid.
[12] TISM, 'How to Get on Alternative Radio', media release, June 1996.
[13] Liz Armitage, 'Spinning into Control', *The Canberra Times*, 19 October 1995, 21.
[14] Andrew Masterson, 'Censorship - Will It All End in Tiers?', *The Age EG*, 2 August 1996, 3.

album's total sales amounted to around 60,000–10,000 off going Platinum.

TISM responded to news of their success with typical satire: 'Naturally we are devastated', they explained. 'For a fiercely ideological, deeply principled band like us to have to put up with screaming teenage girls, celebrities wanting to jam with us, supermodels pestering us for a date – we want the public to know we are really not enjoying ourselves and fame hasn't changed us one little bit.'[15]

TISM themselves felt somewhat bemused by the success of the record, largely utilizing it as a source of fodder for their press interviews in the months and years afterwards. After all, for a band who had thrived away from the intrusion of mainstream attention, the sudden commercial success that came their way brought with it claims of having sold out, or a reduction in quality – something the band vehemently denied.

'We've sort of become more stupid and inane with every year, and I think we've finally found the right formula that everyone seems to like', Hitler-Barassi said in 1996.[16]

He would add in 1998:

It wasn't like we were the critical darlings of the avant garde and suddenly we sold out [. . .] Sure, there might be some people who think that because it's absolutely de rigueur for them that as soon as any album gets in the charts it's gotta be bad. But I've got to say that I don't feel a critical backlash

---

[15] Anon, 'A Sad Event for TISM', *dB Magazine* 358, 29 February 1996.
[16] Tiffany Bakker, 'Who Was That Masked Man?', *TNT* 682, 23 September 1996, 9.

because TISM are suddenly impure, because TISM have never really got a great critical response.[17]

Some journalists even pushed the idea that TISM's moment in the spotlight would go against all they had stood for in terms of mocking the industry itself. The group were far more pragmatic about the notion, however, with Hitler-Barassi noting that their Gold accreditation 'shows me that when we're talkin' at least somebody's listening'.[18]

'I've got no problem with commercial success', he would add. 'This "TISM are a masked bunch of guys who disdain commercial success" is bullshit. I couldn't give a rat's arse about artistic purity. Commercial success equals, to me, a big audience, and I love big audiences.'[19]

Hitler-Barassi expanded on the topic again in 1998:

> The only reason TISM spent years and years and years in the artistic, pure avant-garde is because the mainstream wouldn't have us. But now the mainstream has embraced us, the avant-garde can go stuff themselves as far as we're concerned. For years and years, we've been slagging off the mainstream media, and talking about corporate rock'n'roll and the mendacious entropic forces of world capitalism but that's only because they wouldn't give us any money. The only reason we wouldn't sell our principles was because nobody was buying.[20]

---

[17] Ford, 'Adam Ford Interviews'.
[18] Jenkins, 'Balaclava Road Warriors', 9.
[19] Ford, 'Adam Ford Interviews'.
[20] James Wakelin, 'Behind the Mask', *The Advertiser*, 2 July 1998, 46.

Another, more cynical response was offered by Flaubert following the release of the band's 2002 *Best Off* compilation: 'We're not in it for the art. We're in it for the chicks.'[21]

* * *

In January 1996, TISM released their 'Garbage' single before performing at all legs of the Big Day Out festival for the first time, including their first overseas jaunt by way of a show in Auckland. Many of these shows saw TISM performing either without Hitler-Barassi or with him confined to a wheelchair due to a stage-diving incident at a warm-up show in Lorne, which resulted in an operation to reattach a retina.[22] Though unnecessary for an eye injury, the wheelchair had been used to stop the typically energetic Hitler-Barassi from entering the crowd and further injuring himself. These performances saw TISM utilizing 'giant red phallic inflatables tied to their masked heads',[23] with footage captured and released on the *Ritual Habitual* VHS compilation.

On 27 January 1996, TISM made their debut in triple j's Hottest 100 of 1995 countdown, with '(He'll Never Be An) Ol' Man River', 'Greg! The Stop Sign!!' and 'All Homeboys Are Dickheads' reaching #9, #10 and #93, respectively, making them the first local band to have two placings in the top ten.

---

[21] Eden Howard, 'Good Cleaning Fun', *Rave* 558, 17 September 2002, 14.
[22] Humphrey B. Flaubert, 'TISM on Tour, The Big Day Out: Part Two – The Rest of "Australia"', *Australian Traveller*. http://www.australiantraveller.com/index.cfm?page_id=1276, archived 8 February 2006, at the Wayback Machine.
[23] MTV News Staff, 'Big Day Out Winds Up', *MTV*, 7 February 1996. http://www.mtv.com/news/506977/big-day-out-winds-up/.

This same month also saw TISM return to the studio to record 'a slightly twisted' gospel album 'full of heartfelt tunes and sparse, soulful musicianship'.[24] Dubbed *No Penis – No God*, these recordings would go unheard until the 2009 iTunes release of *www.tism.wanker.com* collected many of them, before the full sessions were released in 2024.

In June, TISM launched their 'You'll Never Walk Again' tour with a one-off show in Auckland, before following it up three months later with three shows in England – their only dates outside of Australasia. Taking place as the result of a grant to export Australian music, more dates were initially planned, including some in Germany, but these failed to come to fruition.

The shows that did take place saw the band performing around London at The Mean Fiddler, Kingston University and the Shepherd's Bush Empire in late September and early October. The Kingston University gig saw the band supporting Carter USM, though the booker of the show was fired as a result of the poor reception.[25] The shows received mixed feelings from the group, with typically chaotic performances making little impact on the foreign crowd.

Despite attempting to win over fans by adopting concepts such as utilizing a Casio with a transmitter to begin their set from within the audience, the shows mainly attracted little more than Australian expats, leaving some members of the

---
[24]TISM, *www.tism.wanker.com* (sleeve notes, Genre B. Goode/Shock Records, 1998).
[25]Mark Pittman, 'I was Responsible for All the UK Shows', Facebook, 21 January 2017. https://www.facebook.com/photo/?fbid=1276278212415697&set=a.1017660651610789&comment_id=1277220165654835.

band feeling as though they'd flown halfway across the world to perform in Melbourne. The ultimate result was effectively an extended holiday for TISM, with minimal performing and copious sightseeing.

Though English audiences would have been exposed to a similar level of dada and social critique through acts such as The KLF,[26] TISM's dreams of international success were likely doomed from the start. Given that more mainstream rock groups such as Midnight Oil and Cold Chisel had failed to break into the American market[27] and Hunters & Collectors unsuccessfully attempted a career in the UK,[28] the chances of TISM's heavily Australian lyrical content and decidedly avant-garde sound finding widespread fame were predictably slim.

During their UK trip, the 1996 ARIA Awards took place in Sydney, with TISM having been nominated for Best Independent Release again, this time for 'Greg! The Stop Sign!!'. The ARIA nomination was ultimately unsuccessful, with You Am I's *Hourly, Daily* taking out the trophy as part of their six-award haul on the night.

In late 1996, the final single from *Machiavelli* was manufactured for release, with copies of 'All Homeboys Are Dickheads' being pressed up and accompanied by two Josh Abrahams remixes of the title track, and a live recording of 'What Nationality Is Les Murray?' from their 1995 Collingwood

---

[26]Though largely referred to as The KLF, the British duo would also release music as The Justified Ancients of Mu Mu/The JAMs and The Timelords, among others.
[27]Tony Sarno, 'Can INXS Break the International Sound Barrier?', *The Canberra Times: Good Weekend*, 27 April 1986, 7.
[28]Ibid., 8.

Town Hall performance. For reasons unknown, this single was never commercially released, with its catalogue number repurposed for their 'Shut Up – The Footy's on the Radio' single in 1997.

In December, the final piece of *Machiavelli* content was released, with a live album of TISM's Collingwood Town Hall performances being issued under the title *Machines against the Rage*.[29] Conceding that 'live albums tend to be exercises in futility that would be too absurd for a Samuel Beckett play', TISM asserted they had upended the concept by delivering 'the first live album recorded entirely in the studio, using only machines'.[30]

While some promotional copies came packaged with the 'All Homeboys Are Dickheads' single, commercial copies saw the live record paired with the *Machiavelli* album – its second reissue in under twelve months. This ploy to capitalize on the success of the record saw *Machines* utilize the same disc artwork, replacing the words 'Popular CD' on *Machiavelli's* disc face with 'Shameless Hollow Publicity Stunt'. When the record was reissued on vinyl in 2022, the four sides of the LPs also bore the titles 'Naked Money Grubbing Exercise', 'Yet More Showbag Tat' and 'Blood? Stone? Done'.

Similarly, in keeping with the fake titles utilized on *Machiavelli*, the live album also featured a fake tracklist, with the first eight tracks dubbed 'The Shit Thing', and the ninth

---

[29] At most dates on the 1996 Big Day Out, TISM performed directly before US outfit Rage against the Machine, effectively seeing their musical machines going against the Rage.
[30] TISM, 'What Is the Point of a Live Album?', media release, December 1996.

and tenth titled 'The Shit Thing, The' and '(The) Shit Thing', respectively.

The live concert itself featured a production of William Shakespeare's *Othello* taking place behind the band during their performance, with the audience being handed a programme which described both the play and the board game of the same name. *Othello*'s theme of race may have also seemed pertinent given the lyrical content of 'Aussiemandias'.

The 1996 release of the performance featured fifteen tracks, of which only three – 'All Homeboys Are Dickheads', 'Aussiemandias' and 'Give up for Australia' – appeared on *Machiavelli*. The 2022 reissue included an additional five tracks, including a diatribe titled 'Ate Breakfast off a Hooker's Tits', and four more songs – 'What Nationality Is Les Murray?', 'Garbage', 'Greg! The Stop Sign!!' and '(He'll Never Be An) Ol' Man River' – all of which originally appeared on the studio album.

The decision to not add them to the initial release is unclear but is likely due to them having already been featured on the studio record also included with the package.

* * *

Though initially slow in gaining mainstream chart success, TISM's rise to the top ten with *Machiavelli* was likely an occurrence the quietly humble band could not have realistically foreseen. While their successes had previously been confined to the underground, the public fascination with TISM that occurred throughout 1995 and into 1996 thrust them into new and unexpected territory.

From top ten chart success to interviews with prominent media personalities, commercial radio airplay, an ARIA Award, airtime on network television and international tour dates, so much was this an unexpected journey that TISM would compile many of these media appearances for their 1998 VHS release, *Gold! Gold!! Gold!!!*.

The most surprising aspect, however, is TISM's own success in spite of themselves. After all, a 1996 press release from the group bluntly stated, 'TISM have done their level best at all times to sabotage their own career'.[31] Fortunately, they failed.

---

[31] TISM, 'Gold! Gold! Gold for Australia!', media release, 5 March 1996.

6 40 years – Then death

Rock and roll is music for the angry and depraved, so you can't really rock and roll 'til you're middle aged. –
'Rebel Without a Paunch' (1998)

For any artist who has experienced even a modicum of success, replicating it can appear as an impossibility. For a band such as TISM, whose mainstream fame was largely impacted by a number of outside factors, the daunting question of where to go next would have presented itself swiftly. However, given that the triumph of *Machiavelli* also resulted from TISM discovering 'the right formula that everyone seems to like',[1] the future may have seemed uncertain. Would it be wise to try and replicate that sound and hope to again achieve mainstream popularity, or would the choice to continue evolving sonically be more gratifying? For TISM, there was no saying both couldn't be true as they ventured towards an unwritten future.

Upon the completion of the *Machiavelli* period in December 1996, TISM made their return in June 1997 with the non-album track 'Shut Up – The Footy's on the Radio'. Peaking at #90 on the charts, November's 'Yob' – the lead single from their next

---
[1] Bakker, 'Who Was That Masked Man?'.

record, 1998's *www.tism.wanker.com* – fared worse with a peak of #118.

Despite what could be considered another commercial misstep by releasing 'I Might Be a Cunt, but I'm Not a *Fucking* Cunt' in April 1998 and pairing it with a sexually explicit music video, TISM again found themselves in the spotlight, this time thanks to a letter from the president of the Victorian Returned & Services League Bruce Ruxton denouncing the single. Their most successful single after *Machiavelli*, 'Whatareya?', would be released in July, with the track peaking at #66.

The release of *www.tism.wanker.com* in June was not paired with as many fortuitous occurrences as its predecessor. While the record again saw the group largely focusing on electronic instrumentation and samples, it didn't climb any higher than its initial chart debut of #26, two months after its release. Despite positive reviews, support from the national Caveat Emptour tour with Regurgitator and The Fauves (who were touring their albums *Unit*[2] and *Lazy Highways*, respectively), and a reputation amongst some members of the band as being their strongest work, the album's time in the spotlight was short-lived.

A two-and-a-half-year period of silence straddled the new millennium, which coincided with TISM's recording their fifth album, *De Rigeurmortis*, released in October 2001 via their new home on the Festival Mushroom Records label. Featuring a similar mix of songs and diatribes as their 1988 *Truckin' Songs*

---

[2] Lachlan Goold and Lauren Istvandity, *Unit* (New York: Bloomsbury Academic, 2022).

album, the record debuted at #24 on the national charts, though it too failed to improve upon its initial performance.

Following the release of their retrospective *Best Off* compilation in late 2002, and Cheese's 2003 solo album *Platter*, the band issued their sixth record, *The White Albun*, in 2004. A deliberate misspelling of The Beatles' 1968 release, it came packaged with two DVDs, including a performance of their 'Save Our TISM' concert at The Hi-Fi Bar in Melbourne in September 2003, and a documentary paired with film clips and music videos. The album would be ineligible for the national chart, instead peaking at #14 on the Australian DVD Chart. The album did, however, receive widespread attention thanks to its only single, 'Everyone Else Has Had More Sex than Me'. Its success was largely due to a film clip from the Australian animator and director Bernard Derriman, which would achieve unexpected virality online, prompting release of the single in Germany, where it charted at #63.

TISM would wrap up their album campaign with a performance at Victoria's Earthcore festival on 27 November 2004. Though unannounced and unplanned, the show would become TISM's last for almost two decades, with the band having silently split the week before.[3] The decision for their final show to be the traditionally electronic Earthcore festival meant the event would see hardly any of their dedicated fans in attendance.

'We did the last tour for the DVD, *The White Albun*, and that went okay, and there was a bit of a debt at the end of

---

[3] Cowell, 'The Birth of Uncool'.

it', remembered Lynch. 'So we ended up doing this show to pay off that debt – the last show – which was Earthcore in November 2004. I think pretty much everyone looked themselves in the eye at the end of it and said, "Well that should do us, shouldn't it?"'[4]

---

[4] Lynch, *The J Files*.

Conclusion

Oh, how does time unnerve us. – 'Lose Your Delusion II' (1995)

In June 1995, those who had witnessed the 'artistic and commercial failure'[1] that was TISM's shambolic first show would likely have had trouble reconciling the band who made their debut at the Duncan Mackinnon Reserve in December 1983 with the same group who had inexplicably landed in the top ten of the ARIA charts with *Machiavelli and the Four Seasons*.

In fact, it's difficult to look at TISM in 1983 and imagine *any* sort of success – mainstream or otherwise – coming their way. Their very existence felt antagonistic, their music lacked any sort of appeal for those outside of their own bedrooms, and they lacked the marketable image of any contemporary rock or pop stars. However, for an avant-garde band whose very approach appeared to revolve around the notion of doing the opposite of what common sense would dictate, it only made sense that a brush with mainstream fame was on the cards.

Even so, the journey from those early days spent making music in their bedrooms to becoming one of Australia's most enigmatic bands with *Machiavelli* is not an entirely linear one. It's one that sees TISM kicking against the pricks of the

---

[1] TISM, *The TISM Guide to Little Aesthetics*, 1.

Australian music industry as they fight for legitimacy with their satirical lyrics, Dadaist approach and pub-rock sound, and one where they contend with making avant-garde pop songs with an entirely non-commercial façade.

Notwithstanding national recognition by way of an appearance on *Hey Hey It's Saturday*, an ARIA Award or spots on the national Big Day Out tour, TISM's wider success still felt confined to their home state. While Flaubert had always dreamed of rock stardom, the only chance of anyone in TISM actualizing such a dream would be by way of a commercial breakthrough – a notion that must have felt like an impossibility.

Although *Machiavelli* is often cited as the moment at which TISM changed their sound, it's a record which arrived as the culmination of everything that had come before it. The seeds of electronic music had been germinating ever since they first utilized a TR-606 instead of a drum kit, and as their collection of instruments grew, so too did a fondness for sampling and genre exploration. Even though two of TISM's members might have wielded a guitar and bass on stage, they were never far from the 'machine-oriented'[2] roots that launched them onto this journey.

However, by the time *Machiavelli* arrived, TISM had indeed experienced years of change. They'd been inspired to move away from the ubiquitous guitar sounds of festival stages and alternative radio, they had experienced line-up changes, and an exposure to contemporary electronic music had shown them a world in which they could thrive. That isn't to say that *Machiavelli* was a drastic change for the group (nor was it an

---

[2] Buttfield, 'Crusaders'.

album they could have made back in the 1980s) but, rather, it was the result of a band following the path they had always been treading and realizing the destinations such a path could lead them.

Those destinations were ultimately some of the most exciting that TISM would ever visit. From national airplay on commercial radio, to widespread press and publicity on network television, to reaching #8 on the ARIA charts and then even winning an ARIA Award, it seemed as though what was impossible just a few short years ago was now a reality. For a brief moment, TISM had become one of the most commanding bands in the country. Their music was undeniably catchy and alluring, and their public persona made them perfect fodder for countless write-ups from bewildered journalists who attempted to crack the enigma that was TISM. It was this confluence of factors that made them irresistible to both music lovers and curious onlookers and placed them in a position desired by almost any artist.

Of course, it's easy to find detractors who will claim that TISM's success was little more than the result of them pulling a fast one on the music industry and the wider public. However, to do so is to undermine their talent and their desire to adapt to a changing musical landscape, to ignore an accomplished album such as *Machiavelli*, and to reduce them to little more than the status of a band who got lucky without putting in the hard yards.

It's just as easy to underline how paradoxical TISM's success was. After all, the very definition of avant-garde refers to experimental art, yet their singular approach would result in appearances alongside some of the music industry's most popular mainstream acts on charts and stages. Those same stages would be graced with TISM's Dadaist live show, where often-divisive performances left audiences unsure of what they were witnessing thanks to the band's myriad concepts and alienating onstage behaviour.

While Dadaism was itself a departure from the norms of traditional art, TISM's embrace of the style was jarring in a musical landscape where the notion of an 'alternative' music scene was in its infancy in the 1980s and still finding mainstream acceptance by the mid-1990s. Resultantly, even those who had found a sense of sanctuary in the comparative open-mindedness of the alternative community would often be shocked by TISM, whose 'firing on all cylinders' approach could be as confrontational as it was intriguing.

Yet, TISM occupied a unique niche within the Australian music scene. Though paradoxically pub rock and avant-garde in their musical approach, their lyrics flirted with popular culture tropes and high culture references, bringing in audiences from all ends of the cultural spectrum. Some people would describe this combination of cultural forms as postmodern. In their wider discography, *Machiavelli* was arguably the album which saw TISM mask their overtly avant-garde approach the most, though it's difficult to say if their resulting success was because of, or in spite of, that fact.

Along with their heavy use of irony and satire, and self-referential songwriting which itself verged on postmodern, the band undeniably drew parallels to categorization-defying names such as Frank Zappa and The Residents, though these artists were typically deeply revered and influential rather than commercially successful.

Perhaps then the greatest parallels could be seen with a group like The KLF, though Flaubert would later joke that given the British electronic duo formed in the late 1980s, TISM were likely an influence on *them*.[3] While The KLF had never actively sought success, their mastery of their craft and nihilistic critique of the music industry resulted in singles which topped global charts and were equally paired with divisive media antics. Following the announcement of their retirement from the music industry in May 1992,[4] The KLF's Bill Drummond and Jimmy Cauty made the controversial decision to burn £1 million in August 1994, going so far as to record the incident and screen it as a film titled *K Foundation Burn a Million Quid* in 1995.

One could argue that TISM were themselves on a similar path following the release of *Machiavelli*. Though their success occurred on a far smaller scale, across a smaller period of time and was largely confined to Australia, TISM could easily have followed suit by departing the music industry in a blaze of glory – making a grand subversive statement about their roles as prominent performers within the business.

Unlike The KLF, however, TISM didn't burn £1 million after *Machiavelli*; rather, they stepped back from the spotlight, content to use their art to comment on what success means within the Australian music industry at the turn of the twenty-first century.

---

[3] Cowell, 'The Birth of Uncool'.
[4] Anon, 'Timelords Gentlemen, Please!', *NME*, 16 May 1992. http://www.libraryofmu.net/display-resource.php?id=309, archived via the Library of Mu.

Perhaps, however, that was part of their plan from the beginning? Though unlikely, it's possible. After all, the best summation of TISM's rise to fame within the 1990s can be provided by Hitler-Barassi, who claimed, 'the greatest satirical statement that we could have made on the Australian rock industry is to actually become moderately successful within it'.[5]

For TISM, *Machiavelli and the Four Seasons* proved that anything was possible – even artistic acceptance by the mainstream.

> *Well. There it is. We are all alone in the end, you know. If only you could help me. But you will never understand.*
> – Liner notes to *Machiavelli and the Four Seasons*.

---

[5] Buttfield, 'The Hitler Diaries'.

Acknowledgements

I extend immense gratitude to my wife, Brittany, for her years spent supporting my endless fanaticism. Thanks, Birdy; your love and charity knows no bounds.

This book could not have been possible without the help of Luke Eygenraam and Brendan Neil. I only wish all music fans were as knowledgeable and dedicated as you both.

Thanks to editor Jon Stratton for his truly inspired insights, and for believing a 33 1/3 Oceania volume on a band like TISM was worth pursuing.

I also acknowledge and appreciate fellow Victims of TISM – including Owen Brown, Robert Carbone, Shane Cubis, Zac Dadic, Luke Devlin, Grant Fleming, Allan Ganzevoort, Mitch Gibson-Kingdom, Jason Kempnich, Mick Packer and Marcus Schmerl – for having allowed me into the world of intense fanaticism with open arms. Richard Miles, you deserve a special mention given the invaluable resource your TISM archives have been.

My thanks to those who helped out in this volume – whether it be by way of inspiration or interviews or by simply providing me with means to access information – including Matt Dower, Ryan Egan, Laurence Maddy, Tony Martin, Lindsay McDougall, Paul McKercher, Chris Penney, Mark Sexton, Adalita Srsen, Tara Thomas, David Thrussell and David Williams.

Of course, immense thanks to all members of TISM, past and present – none of whom were willing to speak about this project on the record. I wouldn't have expected anything less.

This book is also dedicated to the memories of Karyne Jenke, for indirectly introducing me to TISM; Peter Aylward, for his long-time dedication to fanaticism; Kevin 'Yahn Wildebeest' O'Donnell, for putting up with a *lot*; and James Paull, for his years of service – thank you for the music.

Bibliography

Adams, Phillip, *Late Night Live*, Radio National, 9 September 2000.

Anon, '1975-1985: 40 Years of triple j', *The J Files*, Double J, 5 February 2015.

Anon, '1985-1995: 40 Years of triple j', *The J Files*, Double J, 12 February 2015.

Anon, 'A Sad Event for TISM', *dB Magazine* 358, 29 February 1996.

Anon, 'Timelords Gentlemen, Please!', *NME*, 16 May 1992. http://www.libraryofmu.net/display-resource.php?id=309, archived via the Library of Mu.

Anon, 'TISM VS The Beatles', *dB Magazine*, 10 May 1995.

Anon, 'Top Ten Singles: 3PBS Selection', *The Age EG*, 16 May 1986, 6.

ARIA, *The ARIA Report No. 295*, Australian Recording Industry Association, 8 October 1995.

ARIA, 'TISM wins Best Independent Release | 1995 ARIA Awards', YouTube, 4 September 2019. https://www.youtube.com/watch?v=9KAGNUdJvvI.

Armitage, Liz, 'Spinning into Control', *The Canberra Times*, 19 October 1995, 21.

Bakaitis, Mark, 'TISM - UK Tour Promo (1996)', YouTube, 7 April 2014. https://www.youtube.com/watch?v=ew8GTsrsxHI.

Bakker, Tiffany, 'Who Was That Masked Man?', *TNT* 682, 23 September 1996, 9.

Bell, Steve, '20 Years Ago: How TISM's Third Album Helped Them Break Through, Despite Their Best Efforts', *The Music*, 1 May 2015. https://themusic.com.au/features/20-years-ago-tism

-machiavelli-and-the-four-seasons-steve-bell/_fPuERATEhU/01-05-15.

Bennington, Ian, 'Return of the Pop Vigilantes', *Tabula Rasa*, February 2002, 18.

Bruce, David, 'Behind a Band's Mask', *The Age EG*, 23 September 1988, 5.

Butler, Kieran, 'Talcott (3CR) & Ron Hitler Barassi (TISM) 1995', YouTube, 29 August 2016. https://www.youtube.com/watch?v=1QGo0CutT0k.

Butler, Kieran, 'This Is Treachery Sadly - A Podcast with Leak Van Vlalen (TISM)', YouTube, 20 November 2022. https://www.youtube.com/watch?v=NDNMWtdncXg.

Butler, Kieren and Sean Kelly, 'RealiTISM', Station 59, Melbourne, 7 April 2012.

Butler, Kieren and Sean Kelly, 'RealiTISM', Station 59, Melbourne, 14 April 2012.

Buttfield, Brett, 'Crusaders for Citizen Average', *dB Magazine*, 1 March 1995.

Buttfield, Brett, 'The Hitler Diaries', *dB Magazine* 120, 5 June 1996.

Buttfield, Brett. 'Will Success Spoil Hitler-Barassi?', *dB Magazine* 99, 16 August 1995.

Carmine, Ed, 'TISM! How a Balaclava-Clad Band Helped Save the Saints', *Zero Hanger*, 18 February 2022. https://www.zerohanger.com/tism-how-a-balaclava-clad-band-helped-save-the-saints-97849/.

Carter, Peter, 'Saints Set $1.5m Goal to Stay Intact', *The Canberra Times*, 29 June 1995, 22.

Coaltrain, Leonard P., 'TISM Unmasked – Rock'n'Roll Whoppers without the Green Bits', *Revelation* 14, August 1995, 15.

Cohen, Jason and Michael Krugman, *Generation Ecch!: The Backlash Starts Here*, New York: Gallery Books, 1994, 161.

Cohen, Tony and John Olson, *Half Deaf, Completely Mad*, Melbourne: Black Inc., 2023, 166.

Coupe, Stuart, 'Rockers in Caverns Alive and Thriving', *The Sydney Morning Herald*, 20 July 1986, 117.

Cowell, Damian, 'Episode 4: Old Sneakers', *Only the Shit You Love: The Podcast*, 18 August 2021. https://podcasts.apple.com/au/podcast/podcast-3-episode-4-old-sneakers/id1585650286?i=1000535170120.

Cowell, Damian, 'Episode 6: Fucking Annoying', *Only the Shit You Love: The Podcast*, 18 August 2021. https://podcasts.apple.com/au/podcast/podcast-5-episode-6-fucking-annoying/id1585650286?i=1000535170121.

Cowell, Damian, 'Episode 7: The Plot Thins', *Only the Shit You Love: The Podcast*, 8 September 2021. https://podcasts.apple.com/au/podcast/podcast-6-episode-7-the-plot-thins/id1585650286?i=1000535170032.

Cowell, Damian, 'Episode 11: Whatever Happened to Jessie's Girl?', *Only the Shit You Love: The Podcast*, 6 October 2021. https://podcasts.apple.com/au/podcast/podcast-10-episode-11-whatever-happened-to-jessies-girl/id1585650286?i=1000537679311.

Cowell, Damian, 'Episode 12: Don't Bring Me Down, Proust', *Only the Shit You Love: The Podcast*, 13 October 2021. https://podcasts.apple.com/au/podcast/damian-cowell-only-the-shit-you-love-the-podcast/id1585650286.

Cowell, Damian, 'Episode 13: Wot Lionel Ritchie Said', *Only the Shit You Love: The Podcast*, 20 October 2021. https://podcasts.apple.com/au/podcast/podcast-12-episode-13-wot-lionel-ritchie-said/id1585650286?i=1000539134288.

Cowell, Damian, 'Episode 14: Greta the Garbo', *Only the Shit You Love: The Podcast*, 27 October 2021. https://podcasts.apple

.com/au/podcast/podcast-13-episode-14-greta-the-garbo/id1585650286?i=1000539820141.

Cowell, Damian, 'Episode 15: Remember Nostalgia?', *Only the Shit You Love: The Podcast*, 3 November 2021. https://podcasts.apple.com/au/podcast/podcast-14-episode-15-remember-nostalgia/id1585650286?i=1000540575905.

Cowell, Damian, 'Episode 16: Hamster Grammar Rocks Your Party', *Only the Shit You Love: The Podcast*, 10 November 2021. https://podcasts.apple.com/au/podcast/podcast-15-episode-16-hamster-grammar-rocks-your-party/id1585650286?i=1000541293678.

Cowell, Damian, Interview with Zan Rowe, *Take 5*. Double J, 14 September 2018.

Cowell, Damian, 'The Birth of Uncool: How TISM Gatecrashed Melbourne Music', *Vimeo*, 20 March 2014. https://vimeo.com/89629916.

Crocostimpy, Sash, 'Is This Serious, Mum?', *Rip It Up* 308, 9 March 995, 50.

Demetrius, Mark, 'Machiavelli and the Four Seasons', *Rolling Stone Australia* 510, June 1995, 86.

Dwyer, Michael, 'The Phantom Menace', *The Age EG*, 2 July 2004. https://www.theage.com.au/entertainment/music/the-phantom-menace-20040702-gdy5ls.html.

Flaubert, Humphrey B., 'Q&A', *The Herald Sun*, 15 November 2001, 35.

Flaubert, Humphrey B., *The J Files*, triple j, 28 March 1996.

Flaubert, Humphrey B., 'TISM on Tour, The Big Day Out: Part Two – The Rest of "Australia"', *Australian Traveller*. http://www.australiantraveller.com/index.cfm?page_id=1276, archived 8 February 2006, at the Wayback Machine.

Flea, Interview with Francis Leach, *Hi-5*. triple j, 4 May 1996.

Ford, Adam, 'Adam Ford Interviews Ron Hitler Barassi', *Frisbee*, 1998/*Duck Fat* 2, 1999. https://www.oocities.org/tismselfstorage/duckfat.html.

Gold! Gold!! Gold!!!, VHS, edited by Guy Richards, Warner Music, 1998.

Goold, Lachlan and Lauren Istvandity, *Unit*, New York: Bloomsbury Academic, 2022.

Granath, Olle, 'With Andy Warhol 1968', Moderna Museet, Accessed 21 January 2024. https://www.modernamuseet.se/stockholm/en/exhibitions/andy-warhol-other-voices-other-rooms/with-andy-warhol-1968-text-ol/.

Hart, Bob, 'Here's Humphrey', *The Herald Sun*, 21 September 2002, W-02.

Hill, Rachel, 'Shy, Enigmatic, or Just Plain Arrogant?', *The Canberra Times: Good Times*, 16 March 1995, 4.

Hitler-Barassi, Ron, 'James Paull - Tism 1957-2008', *Smartartists Management*. http://www.smartartists.com.au/artists/jock.php, archived 2 May 2008, at the Wayback Machine.

Howard, Eden, 'Good Cleaning Fun', *Rave* 558, 17 September 2002, 14.

Jenke, Tyler, '200 Greatest Australian Albums of All Time', *Rolling Stone Australia* 007, December 2021.

Jenke, Tyler, 'Ex-TISM Member Jack Holt Talks the Debut of His New Band, the Collaborators', *Tone Deaf*, 23 October 2019. https://tonedeaf.thebrag.com/jack-holt-the-collaborators-album-live-interview.

Jenke, Tyler, 'Former TISM Member Jack Holt Unmasks for New Band, the Collaborators', *Tone Deaf*, 3 December 2018. https://tonedeaf.thebrag.com/former-tism-member-unmasks-collaborators/.

Jenkins, Jeff, 'Balaclava Road Warriors', *Inpress* 515, 8 July 1998, 9.

Keats, John, *The Poems of John Keats*, New York: Dodd, Mead & Company, 1905, 195.

Kelly, Sean Anthony, 'I Reckon "Hot Dogma" Suffered from Three Things', Facebook, 7 June 2024. https://www.facebook.com/tismforever/posts/pfbid0ChuQULyhJom2EEivr6Vvvu9VqAvWaTwPywceBarxPP859ux6nMmwndrdqCdLxKnCI?comment_id=474434048494892.

Kelly, Sean Anthony, 'Noble Park Youth Club Dec77?!', Facebook, 20 November 2020. https://www.facebook.com/groups/44545772326/posts/10157643969512327/?comment_id=10157649762007327.

Kingsmill, Richard, 'King Hit - Red Hot Chili Peppers', *triple j*. https://www.abc.net.au/triplej/media/s2306448.htm, archived November 21, 2012, at the Wayback Machine.

Kirby, Michael Jack, 'Hollywood Argyles', *Way Back Attack*, Accessed 16 November 2023. https://www.waybackattack.com/hollywoodargyles.html.

Lynch, Michael, Interview with John Safran, *The J Files*, triple j, 27 August 2015.

Lynch, Michael, *Machiavelli and the Four Seasons*, sleeve notes, Genre B. Goode/Shock Records, 1995.

Mahoney, Maureen, 'Is Litigation the "Suicide Solution"? Performers, Producers and Distributors' Liability for the Violent Acts of Music Listeners', *Touro Law Review* 16, no. 1 (1999): Article 6.

Masterson, Andrew, 'Censorship - Will It All End in Tiers?', *The Age EG*, 2 August 1996, 3.

Mathieson, Craig, 'TISM Break the Ice', *Beat* 216, 17 October 1990.

McKenzie, Simon, 'Begorrah! (Part One)', *Time Off* 729, 12 July 1995.

Moore, Timothy E., 'Scientific Consensus and Expert Testimony: Lessons from the Judas Priest Trial', *Skeptical Enquirer* 20, no. 6 (1996): 37.

MTV News Staff, 'Australian Band "On The Drug That Killed River Phoenix"', *MTV*, 7 June 1995. http://www.mtv.com/news/504382/australian-band-on-the-drug-that-killed-river-phoenix/.

MTV News Staff, 'Big Day Out Winds Up', *MTV*, 7 February 1996. http://www.mtv.com/news/506977/big-day-out-winds-up/.

Murray, Les, *The J Files*, triple j, 28 March 1996.

Oldham, Paul, '"Suck More Piss": How the Confluence of Key Melbourne-Based Audiences, Musicians, and Iconic Scene Spaces Informed the Oz Rock Identity', *Perfect Beat*, January 2014.

O'Neill, David, 'Live Review: This Is Serious Mum?, The Moffs, The Spliffs', *Juke* 635, 27 June 1987.

Osborne, Jerry, 'The Checkered Past of the Hollywood Argyles', *Tampa Bay Times*, 18 April 1997. https://www.tampabay.com/archive/1997/04/18/the-checkered-past-of-the-hollywood-argyles/.

O'Shea, Gerry, 'Vinyl Talk', *The Sydney Morning Herald*, 4 January 1987, 96.

Paull, James, 'Biography', James Paull, 24 April 2008. http://jamespaull.blogspot.com/2008/04/biography.html

Pittman, Mark, 'I was Responsible for All the UK Shows', Facebook, 21 January 2017. https://www.facebook.com/photo/?fbid=1276278212415697&set=a.1017660651610789&comment_id=1277220165654835.

Porteous, Clinton, 'This Is Serious Mum', *Rolling Clone/Lot's Wife*, 20 October 1988, 31.

Porteous, Clinton, 'This Is This Is Serious Mum', *Waves* 81, December 1986.

Purdy, Gavan and Augustus Billy, 'What It Was like to Manage Tism in the 1980s', *Beat Magazine*, 20 July 2021. https://beat.com.au/what-it-was-like-to-manage-tism-in-the-1980s-from-former-manager-gavan-purdy-himself/.

Reynolds, Simon, *Retromania: Pop Culture's Addiction to Its Own Past*, London: Faber & Faber, 2011, ix.

Richter, Hans, *Dada: Art and Anti-Art*, London: Thames & Hudson, 1965, 7.

Sarno, Tony, 'Can INXS Break the International Sound Barrier?', *The Canberra Times: Good Weekend*, 27 April 1986, 7.

Sawford, Gavin, 'You're Only as Jung as You Feel', *Rave* 173, February 1995, 16–17.

Sexton, Mark and John Petropoulous, *TISM #1*, Melbourne: AAARGH! Comics, 1995, 15.

Shoebridge, Neil, 'Radio Man Chases Ratings in a Race against Time', *Australian Financial Review*, 26 February 1996.

Smarelli, Mara, 'Taken for a Ride by Serious Mothers', *The Age EG*, 11 July 1986, 2.

Stratton, Jon, *Human Frailty*, New York: Bloomsbury Academic, 2023, 5.

Stringer, Howard, 'Deep and Meaningless', *Rolling Stone Australia* 424, November 1988.

Stupid Old Channel, 'Matt Meets Music Legend DAMIAN COWELL | Matt Your Heroes', YouTube, 4 March 2021. https://www.youtube.com/watch?v=aEzhWl4SqN8.

Stupid Old Channel, 'Matt Meets St Kilda Legend JUSTIN "FRANKIE" PECKETT | Matt Your Heroes', YouTube, 18 February 2021. https://www.youtube.com/watch?v=4QNbTCIEAAM.

Tate, Senator Michael, 'Mistral Gyro Aire Fans', media release, 25 November 1991.

TISM, *Collected Recordings 1986 - 1993*, sleeve notes, Genre B. Goode/Shock Records, 1995.

TISM, 'Get Fucked Concert', invitation, 1983.

TISM, 'Gold! Gold! Gold for Australia!', media release, 5 March 1996.

TISM, 'Greg! The Stop Sign!!', media release, July 1995.

TISM, 'Hot Dogma: Re-issued And Reconsidered', media release, 22 November 1993.

TISM, 'How to Get on Alternative Radio', media release, June 1996.

TISM, 'I'm on the Drug That Killed River Phoenix', media release, 5 June 1995.

TISM, Junk Mail List, 8 December 1995.

TISM, *Machiavelli and the Four Seasons*, sleeve notes, Genre B. Goode/Shock Records, 1995.

TISM, 'New Single and Album to Be Released Soon', media release, February 1995.

TISM, 'The Art-Income Dialectic', *The White Albun*, Genre B. Goode/Madman, 2004.

TISM, 'The TISM Guide to Literature', media release, 1994.

TISM, *The TISM Guide to Little Aesthetics*, Melbourne: Stock, Aristotle & Waterman, 1989.

TISM, 'TISM and Ken Done: A Timeline', media release, October 1993.

TISM, 'TISM Explained', *The White Albun*, Genre B. Goode/Madman, 2004.

TISM, 'T*I*S*M', media release, July 1985.

TISM, 'TISM Meets Hot Metal', *Hot Metal*, 1995, 26.

TISM, 'TISM's Occasional Pieces', media release, March 1994.

TISM, 'TISM's Reasons to Support American TV', *Underworld* 3, December 1995, 35.

TISM, 'T.I.S.M. - Why??', media release, May 1995.

TISM, 'Top Ten TISM: A Tragicomedy in One Act', *Rolling Stone Australia* 512, August 1995, 25.

TISM, 'What Is the Point of a Live Album?', media release, December 1996.

TISM, 'Who Are TISM?', *TISM*. http://www.tism.com.au/whoaretism/frames.html, archived 6 December 2000, at the Wayback Machine.

TISM, *www.tism.wanker.com,* sleeve notes, Genre B. Goode/Shock Records, 1998.

Transport Accident Commission Victoria, '"Darren" Country Kids TAC tv ad', YouTube, 2 December 2009. https://www.youtube.com/watch?v=zXiyFkJMAPI.

Tulich, Katherine, 'Triple J Leads A Radio Revolution', *Billboard*, 30 September 1995, 63–4.

Underwood, Alex, 'Looking back at Melbourne's "Little Band Scene"', *Pilerats*, October 2016. http://pilerats.com/music/bands/looking-back-at-melbournes-little-band-scene/.

Van Taylor, David, di., *Dream Deceivers,* 3-D Documentaries, 1992.

Wakelin, James, 'Behind the Mask', *The Advertiser*, 2 July 1998, 46.

Walker, Clinton, *Stranded: The Secret History of Australian Independent Music 1977–1991*, Sydney: Pan Macmillan, 1996, 190.

Williams, David Roy, *This Is Serious Mum,* sleeve notes, Genre B. Goode/DRW, 2021.

Zwar, Adam, 'TISM'S Damian Cowell', *Out of the Question with Adam Zwar*, 16 December 2015. https://omny.fm/shows/10-questions-with-adam-zwar/10-questions-with-adam-zwar-tisms-damian-cowell.

Index

'!UOY Sevol Natas'   75–7, 110
'(He'll Never Be An) Ol' Man
    River'   9, 54, 59–65, 71, 84,
    87, 94, 101, 105, 110, 119,
    122, 126
3PBS   89
3RRR   4, 28–9, 50, 89

AAARGH! Comics   115
Abroz   11
'Abscess Makes The Heart Grow
    Fonder'   105–6
accreditation   9, 108, 119–21,
    see also Gold; Platinum
AC/DC   12, 61, 106, 114
AFL   4, 23–4, 84, 91, 124–5
'All Homeboys Are
    Dickheads'   65–8, 76, 88,
    122, 124–6
alternative   1, 37, 46, 69, 114,
    118–19, 134, 136
anti-art   20
art-rock   22
'Aussiemandias'   43, 94–7, 110,
    126
Austereo   118

Australasian Performing Right
    Association (APRA)   6
Australia the Lucky Cunt   41,
    110
Australian Broadcasting
    Corporation (ABC)   1, 98,
    113, 118
Australian Recording Industry
    Association (ARIA)
    (Awards)   9, 30, 36, 40–1,
    65, 79, 84–7, 113–14, 117,
    124, 126, 133–5
Australian Rules Football   4,
    23–4, 84, 91, 124–5
avant-garde   20–1, 24, 120–1,
    124, 133–6

Barassi, Ron   45–6
Barnard, Rebecca   31
'Bash This Up Your Ginger'   109
Bass   5, 14, 16, 49, 61, 63–4, 72,
    74, 91, 101, 134
Beach Boys, The   81
Beasts of Bourbon   38, 40
Beasts Of Suburban, The   24,
    38, 40–1, 47, 55, 71, 109

Beatles, The   88, 102–3, 131
Berry, Chuck   6, 103
Best Off   18, 122, 131
Big Day Out   41, 45–7, 102, 109, 122, 125, 134
Big Pig   19, 29
Billy Thorpe & the Aztecs   8
Birthday Party, The   15, 40, 98
Blackman, Tokin' (a.k.a. Tony Coitus)   5–6, 31, 38–9, 61, 73, 75, 77, 82, 88, 91, 100–1, 106–7
Bourke, Pieter   52, 71–2, 93–4, 107
Boyz 'N the Hoods   66
Brecht, Bertold   20, *see also* Brechtian

Caligula   47
Captain Beefheart   21
Carter USM   47, 123
Cave, Nick   15, 39, 68, 109
Chapman, Barry   118
Cheese, Jock   5–7, 14–15, 18, 21, 61, 65, 81, 86, 91, 131
Cohen, Tony   38–41, 77
Coitus, Tony (a.k.a. Tokin' Blackman)   5–6, 31, 38–9, 61, 73, 75, 77, 82, 88, 91, 100–1, 106–7
Collaborators, The   6

Collected Recordings 1986–1993   35, 38, 40, 43, 77, 117
Collected Versus   2
Collingwood (Collingwood Town Hall)   33, 38, 110, 124–5
comics   7, 59, 108, 115–16
commercialism   8–9, 22–3, 27–9, 38, 54, 59, 65, 102, 113, 116, 118–21, 125–6, 130, 133–4, 136
controversy   9, 42, 45, 62–3, 65, 87–8, 118, 137
Cosmic Baby   50
costumes   3, 20, 26–7, 32, 33, 86
Cummings, Stephen   100, *see also* The Sports

Dadaism   20, 29, 134, 136
dance music   9, 47, 48, 50, 59, 71–2
DC3, The   6, 47
de la Hot-Croix Bun, Eugene   5–6, 13–14, 16, 18, 22, 48, 49, 51, 71, 88, 93
De Rigeurmortis   130
'Defecate on My Face'   28, 30, 73
Devo   21–2
diatribe   4–5, 30, 41, 60, 65–7, 81, 105–10, 116, 126, 130
'Dicktatorship'   106

disco   12, 49–50
'Does Fame Bring Forth Madness?'   106, 109
Done, Ken   41–2, 103
'"Don't Believe the Hype" Is Hype'   67, 109
doo-wop   8, 55–7, 81
Dostoevsky, Fyodor   68
Double J.   118
drums/drum machine   4, 12, 27, 32, 45, 48–9, 51–2, 61, 65–6, 72, 88, 96, 106, 134

Earthcore   131–2
electronic music   46, 48, 50, 52, 77, 93, 98, 107, 114, 130, 131, 134, 137
Elliot, 'Mama' Cass   61
Elvis Records   28, 30
Eno, Brian   48, 114
experimental   12, 15, 22, 52, 135

Fauves, The   86, 99, 130
festival   41, 45–7, 60, 81, 102, 109, 122, 125, 131–2, 134
Flaubert, Humphrey B.   4, 6, 7, 11–17, 22–3, 25, 27, 31, 33, 37, 45–51, 53, 55, 59, 62, 64–6, 70, 72, 74, 78, 85–6, 88, 91, 93, 96, 98, 104, 114–16, 122, 134, 137
Flea   63–4

Form and Meaning Reach Ultimate Communion   29

'Garbage' (Original)   69–73, 77, 103, 107, 122, 126
'Garbage' (Remix)   71–2
Genre B. Goode (Label)   53, 57
Genre B. Goode (Musician)   6, 26
Get Fucked Concert   26–7
'Give Up For Australia'   97–100, 126
Glass, Philip   99–101
Go-Betweens, The   100–1, *see also* McLennan, Grant
Gold   9, 108, 119, 121, *see* accreditation; Platinum
Gold! Gold! Gold for Australia!   108–9
Gold! Gold!! Gold!!!   80, 127
'*Great Truckin*' Songs of the Renaissance   9, 18, 29–30, 35, 38, 130
'Greg! The Stop Sign!!'   9, 65, 71, 80–7, 101, 103, 106–7, 117, 122, 124, 126
grunge   8, 46–7
guitar   5, 8, 12–14, 16, 18, 31, 38–40, 43, 47, 61, 66, 73, 75, 77, 82, 88, 91, 93, 106–7, 110, 134
Guns N' Roses   73–4

Harris, Rolf 98
Hey Hey It's Saturday 3, 30, 134
hip-hop/rap 66–8, 88, 106, 114
Hitler, Adolf 4, 24, 28
Hitler-Barassi, Ron 4–6, 10, 17, 21, 23–6, 32–3, 37, 39, 41, 46, 49, 55, 60, 62–4, 66–7, 75, 83, 86, 88, 91, 93, 95–6, 98, 101, 103, 106–10, 115–16, 120–2, 138
Hollywood Argyles, The 8, 54–5
Hot Dogma 35–9, 45–7, 51–2, 90, 99–100
Hottest 100 9, 65, 87, 101, 122
'How Do I Love Thee?' 89–90
humour 1, 4, 17, 23, 25, 28, 92
Hunters & Collectors 14, 124

I Can Run 15, 16, 18, 22, 26, 89
'If You Ever Hear His Name, Harden Not Your Arteries' 109
irony 10, 32, 53, 55, 70, 83, 94, 107, 114, 136
iTunes 98, 103, 123

Jackson, Michael 61, 108
Johnny Otis Show, The 65, 76
Judas Priest 75–6
Jung, Carl 91
'Jung Talent Time' 43, 52–3, 71, 90–4
'Junk' 71–2

Keating, Paul 40, 82, 102
Kestrel Hawk 11–12, 14
keyboard 5, 13, 16, 36, 48–9, 71, 93, 106
KLF, The 124, 137
Ku Klux Klan 3, 20, 26

'Last Soviet Star, The' 41, 102–4
Led Zeppelin 11–12, 110
Lennon, John 3, 88, 102
Little Band Scene 12–13, 15, 30
'Lose Your Delusion II' 73–5, 133
L'Touzin 18
Lynch, Michael 22, 28, 56, 57, 72, 92–4, 103, 132

Machiavelli and the Four Seasons 8–9, 36, 43, 45–8, 50–1, 54–5, 57, 65, 67, 69, 72, 74, 77–8, 81, 94, 99, 102, 104, 107–9, 113–14, 117, 124–6, 129–30, 133–8
Machiavelli, Niccolò 55, 101

Machines against the Rage 125
Maddy, Laurence 7, 35–6, 40, 46, 51–2, 71, 102
Martin, Tony 7, 86–7
masks 1–3, 6, 7, 32–3, 121–2
McCartney, Paul 101–2
McKercher, Paul 7, 43, 46
Melbourne 1, 4, 8, 12–13, 15, 17, 23–4, 26–30, 38, 51, 54–5, 60, 63, 89, 100–2, 124, 131
Metallica 76
Metropolis Studios 43
Milli Vanilli 47, 113
Minogue, Kylie 91, 108
Miserables, Les 5–6, 26
Murray, Les 74, 77–80, 124, 126
music producer/music production 7, 35–6, 38–40, 43, 51–4, 66, 114
Musicland Independent Distributors 30, 35

New Order 48
New Waver 109

O'Connor, Sinéad 42

Painters and Dockers 28
parody 56, 81, 88, 93–4, 103, 114

Paxton, Gary S. 54–5
Petropoulos, John 115–16
Phoenix, River 10, 60, 62–5, 119
Phonogram 35, 37
Platinum 120, *see* accreditation; Gold
Platinum Studios 40, 51, 102, 114
Platter 131
'Play Mistral For Me' 66–7, 87–8, 110
Polygram 35, 37
pop music 8–10, 15–16, 21–3, 30, 39, 50, 56, 69, 90–1, 100, 133, 134
Pop Will Eat Itself 47, 65
post-punk 12–13, 15, 22, 24, 48
Primitive Calculators 13
Prince of Wales 28, 31
Public Enemy 67
pub-rock 8, 28, 134, 136
Purdy, Gavan 15, 28, 36, 111

racism 67, 95–6
Radio 4, 9, 30, 56, 61, 63, 89, 118–19, 125–6, 129, 134–5
Rage Against The Machine 125
Rebecca's Empire 31

Red Hot Chili Peppers   63–4
Remix   41, 52, 71–2, 93–4, 108, 124
Residents, The   19–23, 136
Roland   27, 48–9
Rolling Stone Australia   2, 9, 30, 36, 114–15
Root!   6
'Rubbish'   71–2

sampling   4, 8, 39, 47–9, 51, 65–6, 72, 76, 78, 96–8, 130, 134
satanic panic   75–7
satire   2, 10, 25, 30, 40, 43, 59, 64, 68, 74, 79, 93, 114–15, 120, 134, 136, 138
SBS   74, 78–9, 85
Scott, Bon   61
Serious Young Insects   16, 27
Sexton, Mark   7, 108, 115–17
Shakespeare, William   106, 110, 126
Shock Records   7, 38, 42, 53–4, 115
Sly and the Family Stone   94–5
Snog   52–3, 71, 92–4
soccer   77–9, 88
Soundgarden   45–6
Springvale   12, 24, 57, 59
St Kilda   3, 24, 28, 66, 86, 108
St. Peenis, Jon   5–6

'Strictly Loungeroom'   71, 106–7
'Strictly Refuse'   71, 107
suburbia   12, 17, 24, 26, 55, 57, 59, 83
synthesizer   8, 49, 61, 65, 71, 74–7, 98, 106

Tall Stories   14–15, 18, 22
techno   43, 46–9, 52, 56, 59, 61
Thrussell, David   7, 52–3, 71–2, 92–4, 107
TISM Guide to Little Aesthetics, The   36, 68
trance   50, 74, 84
triple j   9, 42–3, 54, 63–5, 79, 87, 101–2, 113, 118–19, 122
Triple M.   118–19

Valli, Frankie (the Four Seasons)   55
Van Vlalen, Leak   5–6, 11–12, 14, 16, 18, 21, 36

Warhol, Andy   90–1
Warner, Dave (From The Suburbs)   21, 24
'What Nationality Is Les Murray?'   74, 77–80, 124, 126
White Albun, The   111, 131
White, Mark   16, 27

Williams, David   7, 27, 42,
   47–8, 56, 58, 62, 84, 103, 119
Wilmot, Greg   14, 18
www.tism.wanker.com   99,
   123, 130

Yankovic, 'Weird Al'   25
Young Talent Time   91

Zappa, Frank (The Mothers of
   Invention)   21, 56, 136

www.ingramcontent.com/pod-product-compliance
Lightning Source LLC
LaVergne TN
LVHW022101240725
817018LV00003B/95